I0797976

# MUSHROOMS

## AND COMPANY

First published in English by Greystone Books in 2025
Originally published in Dutch in 2023 as *Paddenstoel & co: Hoe een schimmelig netwerk het leven op aarde overeind houdt* by Uitgeverij J.H. Gottmer/H.J.W.


25 26 27 28 29   5 4 3 2 1



Greystone Kids / Greystone Books Ltd.
greystonebooks.com

Cataloguing data available from Library and Archives Canada
ISBN 978-1-77840-222-7 (cloth)
ISBN 978-1-77840-223-4 (epub)

Editing by Linda Pruessen
Copy editing by Dawn Loewen
Proofreading by Alison Strobel
Indexing by Stephen Ullstrom
Cover and interior design of the Dutch edition by Wendy Panders
The illustrations in this book were rendered in fineliner and fountain pen and colored digitally

Interior photos © Shutterstock.com: **13** Connie Pinson; **33** Tawan Photo Studio; **34** Pong Wira; **54** Nataliia Yankovets; **57** Mateusz Sciborski; **63** Roman Kalishchuk; **67** Edwin Butter; **85** SandaloFilms; **90** Nata Naumovec; **93** Janny2; **103** Palephotography; **109** Helen Kattai; **127** macro.viewpoint

Scientific review by Andy MacKinnon

Printed and bound in China on FSC® certified paper at Shenzhen Reliance Printing. The FSC® label means that materials used for the product have been responsibly sourced.

Greystone Books thanks the Canada Council for the Arts, the British Columbia Arts Council, the Province of British Columbia through the Book Publishing Tax Credit, and the Government of Canada for supporting our publishing activities.

The publisher gratefully acknowledges the support of the Dutch Foundation for Literature.

EU Safety Information: Easy Access System Europe, Mustamäe tee 50, 10621 Tallinn, Estonia, gpsr.requests@easproject.com

Canada

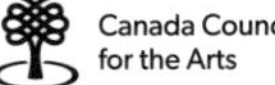
Canada Council for the Arts  Conseil des arts du Canada

Nederlands letterenfonds dutch foundation for literature

**Greystone Books gratefully acknowledges the xʷməθkʷəy̓əm (Musqueam), Sḵwx̱wú7mesh (Squamish), and səl̓ilwətaɬ (Tsleil-Waututh) peoples on whose land our Vancouver head office is located.**

GEERT-JAN ROEBERS · ILLUSTRATED BY WENDY PANDERS
TRANSLATED BY MICHELE HUTCHISON

# MUSHROOMS AND COMPANY

## How a Marvelously Moldy Network Supports Life on Earth

GREYSTONE KIDS
GREYSTONE BOOKS • VANCOUVER / BERKELEY / LONDON

FOLLOW ME

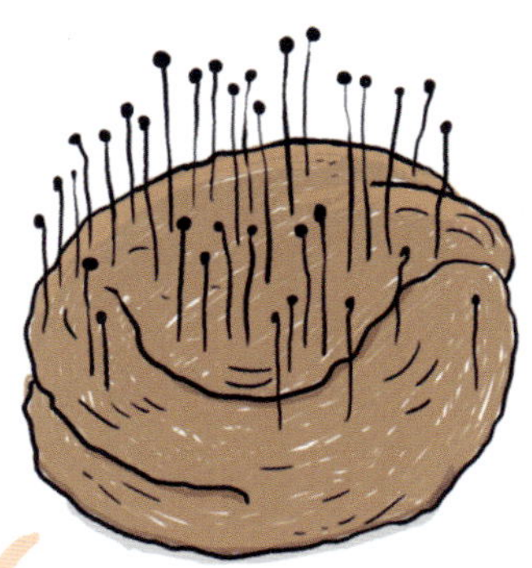

This book is full of mushrooms, but the purple ones like this are special: they contain a bit of extra reading. The text in the purple mushrooms might be more complicated than the main text, and it is always bonus information. If you want to read on, you can just skip them. Unlike real mushrooms, they don't disappear, so you can always read them later if you feel like learning more.

**Difficult words**

Some **words** are printed in a different color and/or size from the rest. These are often more technical words, but never fear! All of them are defined in the glossary at the back of the book. So if there's a word you don't understand and you can't find where it was first explained, just look it up there.

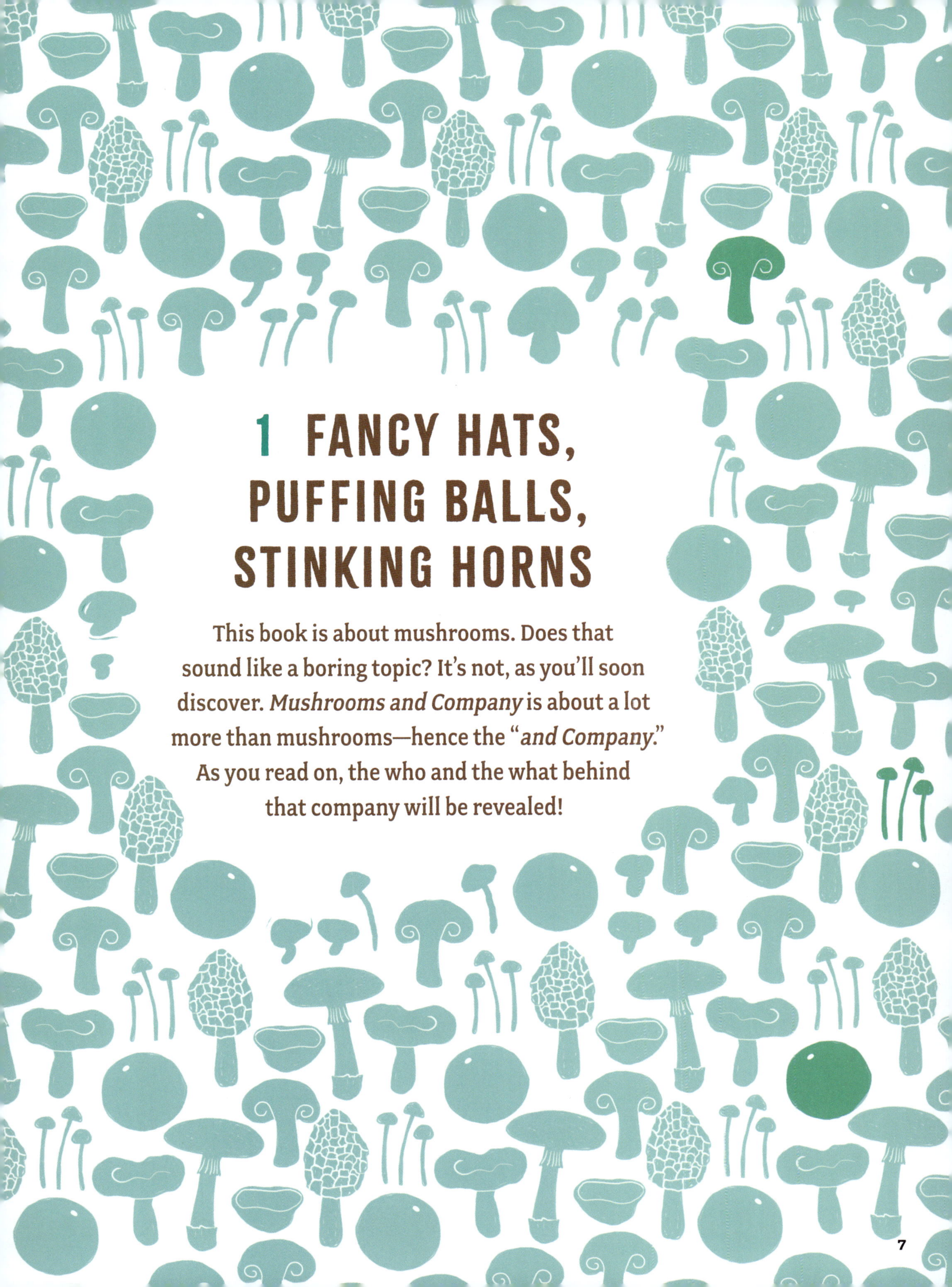

# 1 FANCY HATS, PUFFING BALLS, STINKING HORNS

This book is about mushrooms. Does that sound like a boring topic? It's not, as you'll soon discover. *Mushrooms and Company* is about a lot more than mushrooms—hence the "*and Company*." As you read on, the who and the what behind that company will be revealed!

# First impressions

What springs to mind when you think about **mushrooms** and toadstools? Kindergarten, probably—when you might have crafted toadstools from empty toilet paper rolls. And fairies, and walks in the woods in autumn. A mushroom is a nice detail in a forest, a decorative dwarf under the sturdy wooden giants. But amazingly, without mushrooms, trees wouldn't exist. More amazingly still, there would probably be life only in the sea. Yes, it's true: The fact that you're even reading this book is thanks to mushrooms. And not because the book wouldn't have anything in it without them, but because human beings wouldn't have evolved without their help.

**The word "toadstool" is often used to refer to poisonous mushrooms like the fly agaric, while mushroom tends to be used for the edible types. But there's really no difference between the two.**

HELLO

fly agaric

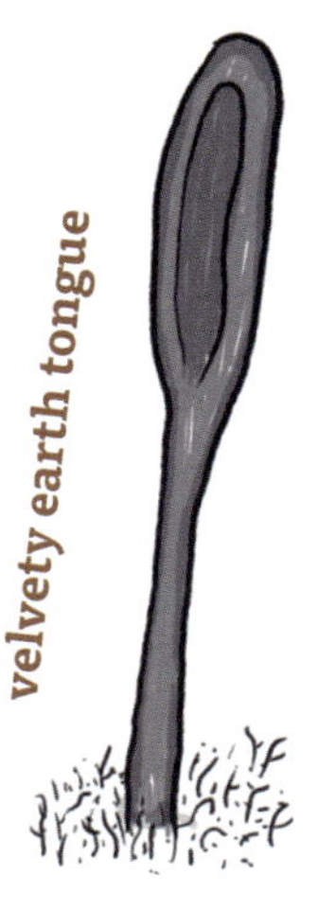

## From witch to where?

You probably think mushrooms are nice to look at, and you definitely find them interesting, or you wouldn't be reading this book. But not everyone likes them. In the Middle Ages, most people hated them. Back then, mushrooms were associated with witches and the devil.

Some people still think they are weird, yucky, and dangerous. But most people don't think about them at all. They spot a few when taking a walk in the autumn and don't give them another thought for the rest of the year. To them, mushrooms are unimportant, ugly, and uninteresting. How wrong they are!

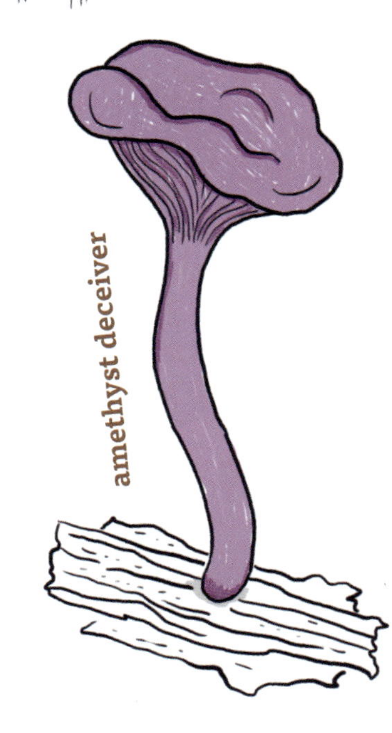

# Pavement mushrooms and more

More good news: If you want to see mushrooms and you live in Canada or the United States, you're in the right place. There are around 11,000 recorded species here. It might not be autumn, but that doesn't matter: you can find them all year round. Elf cups pop up in the early spring, and witch's butter love the winter. (With the scientific name *Tremella mesenterica*, it's perhaps no surprise that witch's butter "tremble" in the freezing cold!)

Don't feel like going into the woods? No problem. You can find mushrooms in the city too. That's how the pavement mushroom got its name. You can find mushrooms almost anywhere! The witch's hat grows on lawns, the deceiver likes forests, the fairy ring mushroom likes fields, and the *dune* brittlestem lives, well, just where you think it might.

# Strange shapes, funny names

Looking at mushrooms never gets boring. They have funny shapes. Even the basic mushroom with its stem and sombrero is quite special. And their names are sometimes even funnier. Some of them still have a touch of medieval superstition to them. Others are kind of cute or nice, and a few more are a little spooky, or might make a good insult.

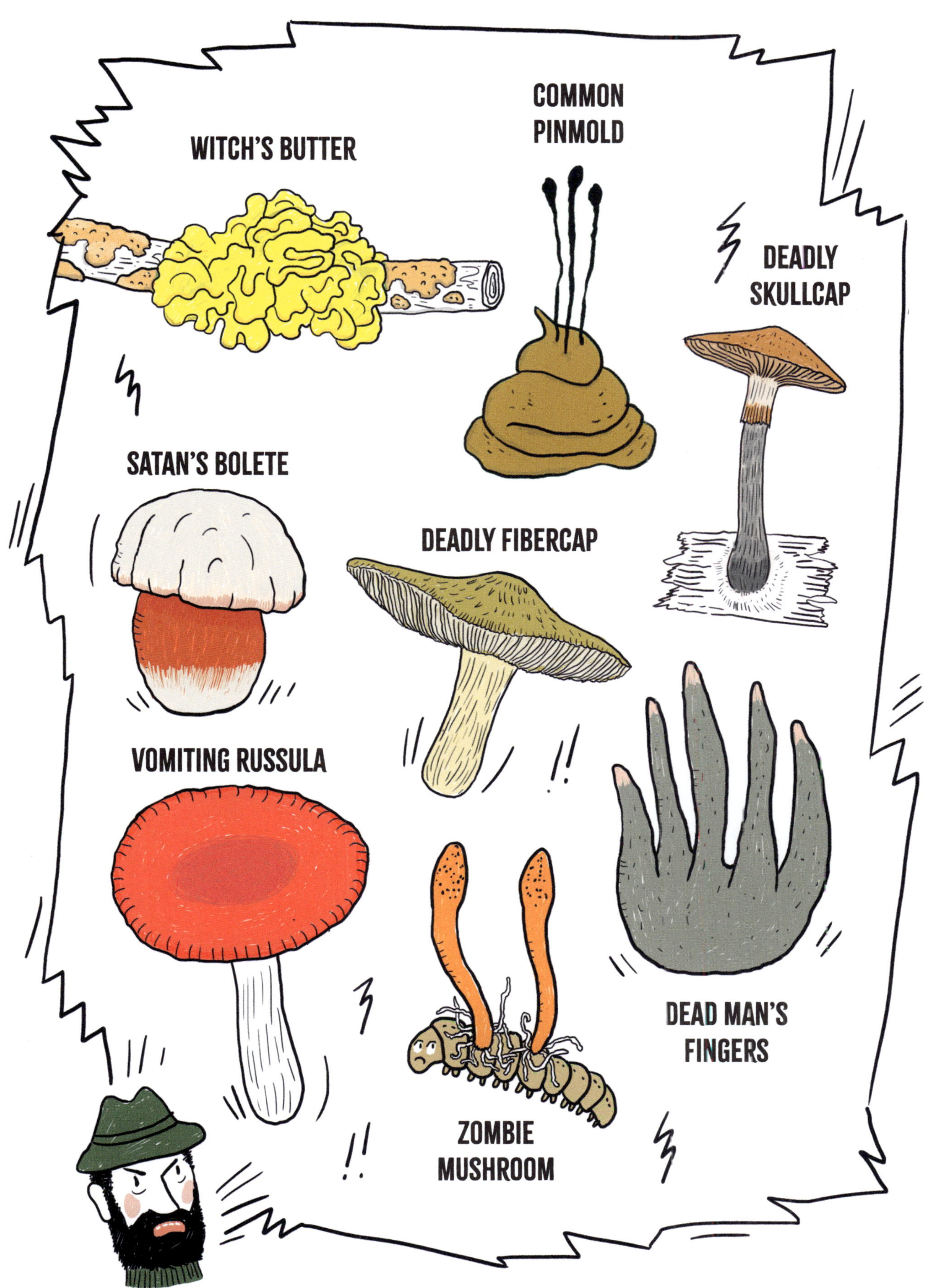
WITCH'S BUTTER
COMMON PINMOLD
DEADLY SKULLCAP
SATAN'S BOLETE
DEADLY FIBERCAP
VOMITING RUSSULA
DEAD MAN'S FINGERS
ZOMBIE MUSHROOM

## Lots of different names

Here are some strangely shaped mushrooms. And yes: the names can be strange too. All mushrooms have scientific names in Latin that can be used in any country, and most also have "common names" in whatever regions they are found. We will use the scientific name only when there isn't also an English common name.

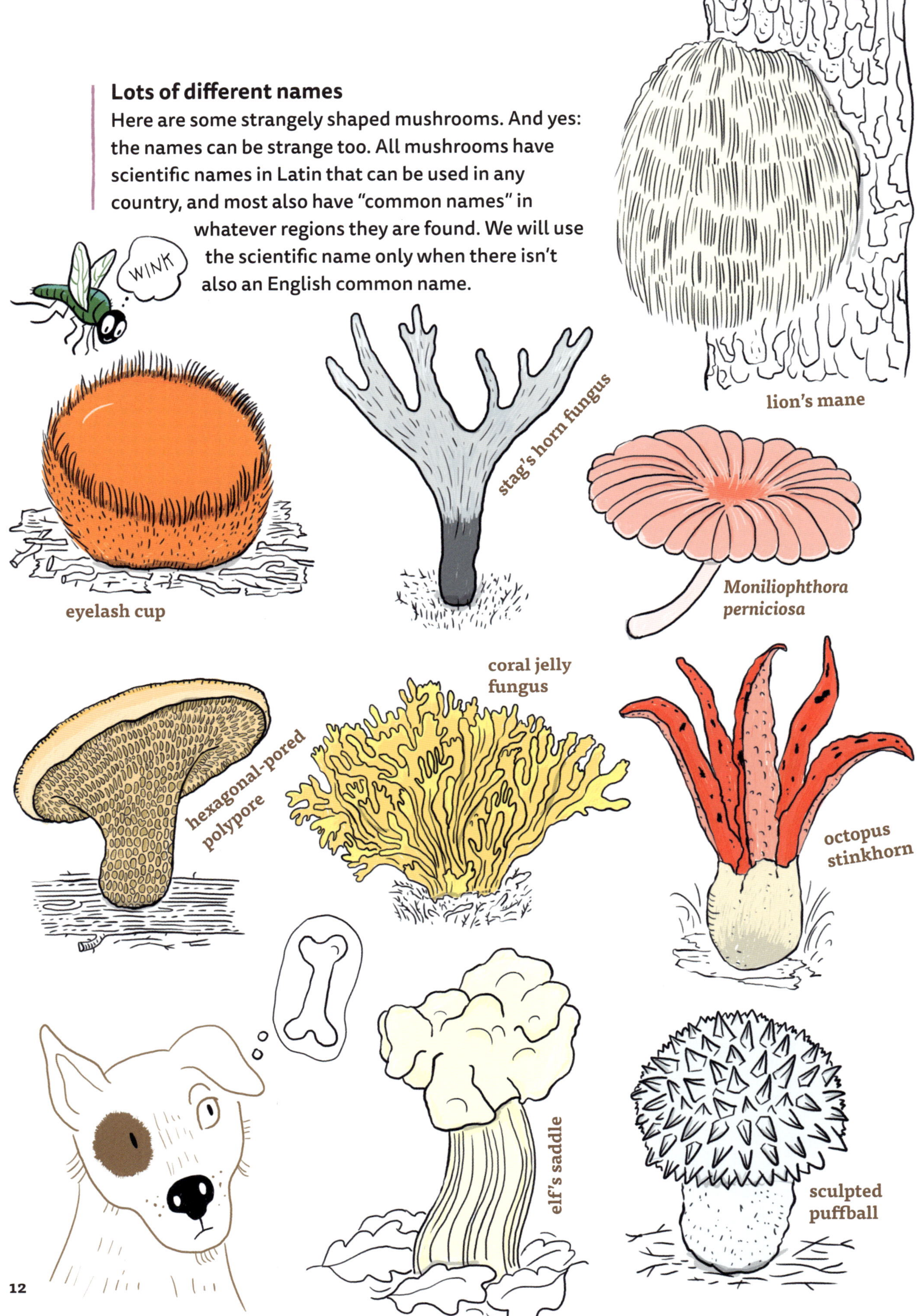

Name: **veiled lady** | Scientific name: ***Phallus indusiatus***

The beautiful tropical cousin of the stinkhorn. Wearing a lovely bridal gown and disgusting perfume. Well, for humans, at least. Flies are very attracted to the smell.

# Fantastic facts

There's a lot to be said about mushrooms. Let's start with a fantastic fact.

You've probably already heard of fireflies, as well as deep-sea fish with lights on their heads. But did you know there are also mushrooms that give off light? In tropical rainforests there are species that light up enough for you to be able to read this book at night. We don't have those kinds of reading lamps in North American and European forests, but if you dare go into the woods on a dark, dark night, you might see a jack-o'-lantern mushroom shining away. That particular mushroom is quite rare, but honey fungi aren't. They grow in almost every forest, and the threads that make up their underground network glow on warm summer nights. Cool, right?

jack-o'-lantern mushroom

PARTY?

honey fungi

## A couple more fantastic facts

Not all mushrooms are dwarfs . . .

- In Kew Gardens near London in the United Kingdom, there is an elm tree with a giant elm bracket growing on its trunk. That particular mushroom has a circumference of more than 16 feet (5 meters).
- Mushrooms with a cap 3 feet (1 meter) wide grow from termite hills in Africa. If they were dining tables, you could fit six chairs around them.
- Many giant puffballs are the size of a football and some are the size of a basketball, but the record holder was as big as a large beach ball. These giants grow in fields and along the sides of roads.

**. . . but there are dwarfs among them:**

- The alder webcap's hat is as small as the nail on your little finger.
- You need a microscope to see some mushrooms. And you wouldn't really be able to call them toadstools because they are much too small for even a tiny toad to sit on.

alder webcap

dark honey fungus

**Mushrooms pop up and disappear again, but the fungus lives on under the ground. Some for a very long time.**

- A honey fungus from Oregon in the United States is estimated to be at least 2,000 years old—but 8,000 is also possible. Unfortunately, mushrooms don't keep track of their age.

**Mushrooms can explode.**

- Some shoot out their "children" at a speed of 375 miles per hour (600 kilometers per hour). Not even a Formula 1 driver would be able to keep up.

white truffle

**The price of some mushrooms will make your eyes pop.**

- As you know, you can eat some mushrooms, which is why you can buy them in shops. A half-pound (225-gram) tub of button mushrooms costs a couple of dollars in the supermarket. But in 2010, a chef paid 105,000 euros (about US$140,000) for a white truffle weighing less than 2 pounds (1 kilogram). At the time, he could have bought over 6 pounds (almost 3 kilograms) of gold for that price—but gold isn't as tasty and it makes a bit of a heavy meal!

# What this book is actually about

You're already at the end of the first chapter and the most important thing hasn't even been explained yet: what mushrooms are. Well, to be honest, that was deliberate. It's also a little fuzzy in the book's title (that "*and Company*" again!) because what mushrooms are sounds kind of gross. Actually, this book is about

**Is a mushroom a type of fungus, then? Yes. Or better still, it's part of a fungus.**

**Did you know that mold is also a type of fungus? You probably know mold as**

- The nasty spots on a forgotten sandwich
- The bluish-green dust on rotten oranges
- The mysterious growths in the organic waste bin

A **mold** is the furry growth of tiny funguses (or "fungi") you find in warm, damp places, usually on food or other organic matter.

The fungus that a mushroom belongs to is bigger than the mushroom itself. In fact, it's often as big as a tree trunk, and sometimes even bigger than a soccer pitch. So why have you never seen these giant monsters? Because they are hidden as tiny threads under the ground. Or in the wood of a dead tree. Or a living one. Fungi grow wherever there's something for them to do. And mainly, something for them to eat.

# Into the depths

But we're getting ahead of ourselves. Maybe you've never realized that molds are alive and related to mushrooms. Let alone that they eat. And poop and search and hunt and tease and make plans, work together, and . . . sorry, too fast again. Before we get into all of that, let's take a look around the world *under* a mushroom, in the secret kingdom where molds reign. Because yes, under the ground they are the boss. Worms, moles, centipedes, even the roots of trees and other plants are all supporting players, ruled over by King Fungus. Keep reading to find out more . . .

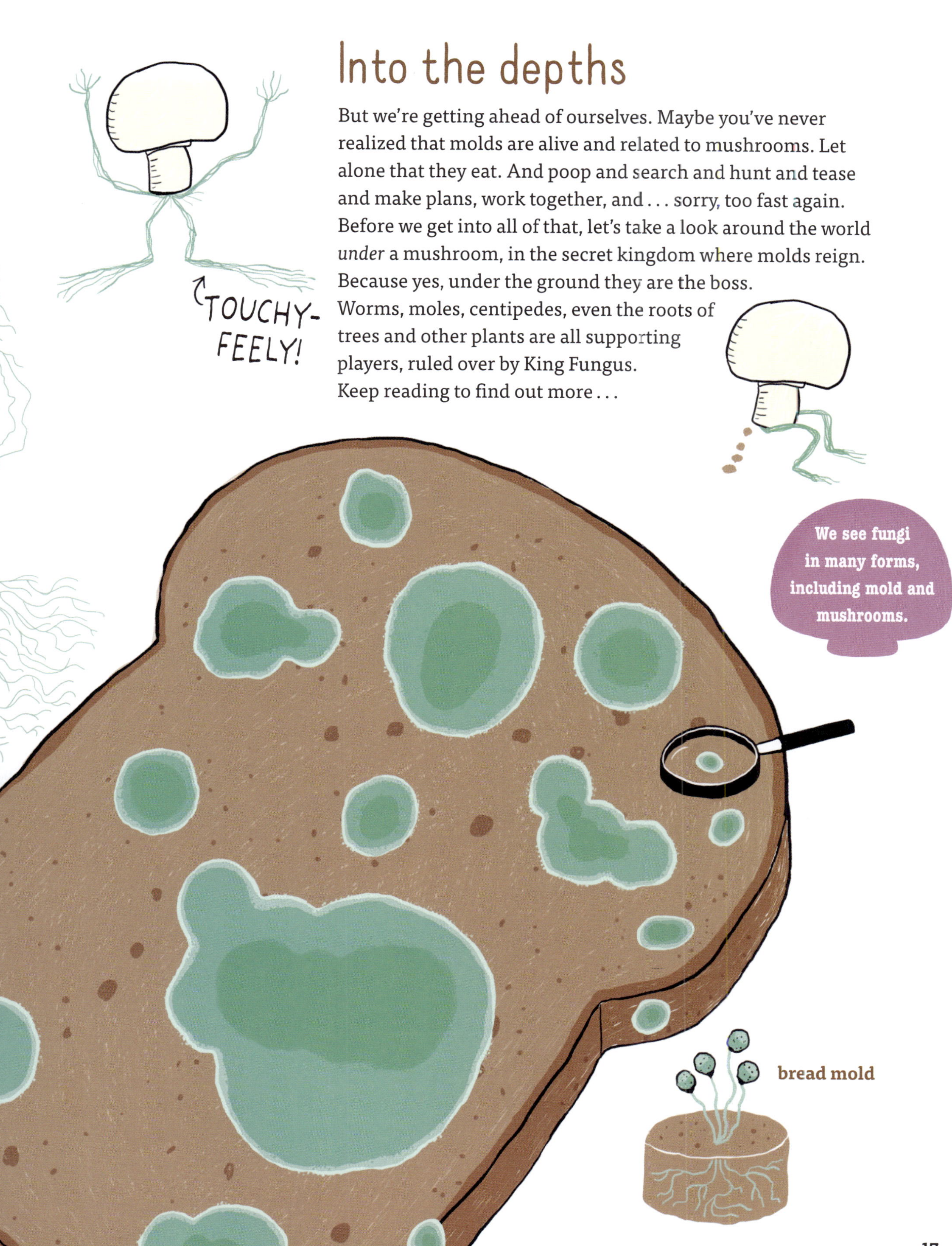

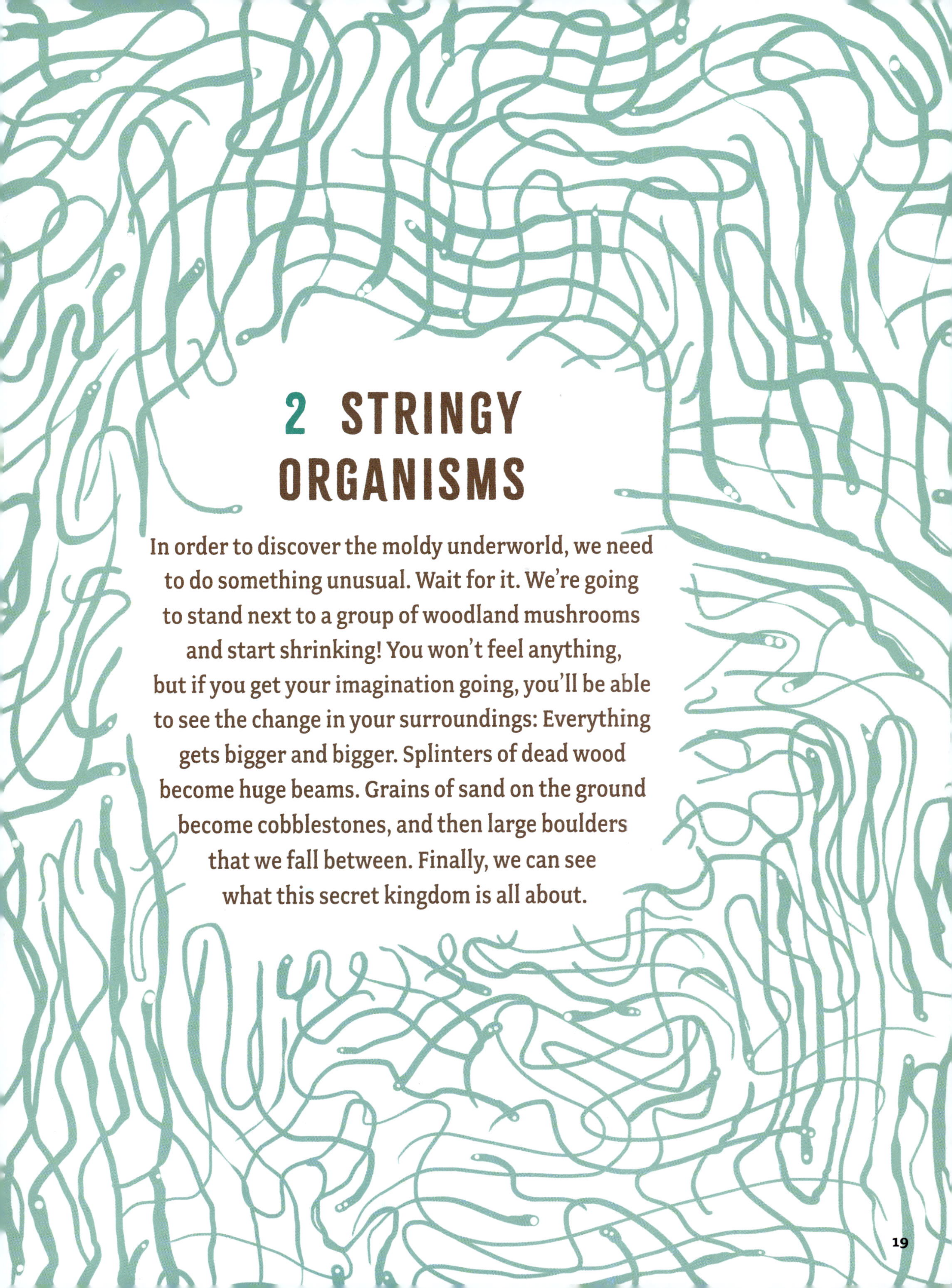

# 2 STRINGY ORGANISMS

In order to discover the moldy underworld, we need to do something unusual. Wait for it. We're going to stand next to a group of woodland mushrooms and start shrinking! You won't feel anything, but if you get your imagination going, you'll be able to see the change in your surroundings: Everything gets bigger and bigger. Splinters of dead wood become huge beams. Grains of sand on the ground become cobblestones, and then large boulders that we fall between. Finally, we can see what this secret kingdom is all about.

# The world under the mushroom

Look: Countless pale threads grow throughout the soil, crisscrossing and connecting. They form a large network. And each thread is attached to several mushrooms. All together, that network of threads is much larger than the group of mushrooms. The mushrooms we saw before we shrank were the tip of the "fungal beast" we're now standing on. Is it a many-headed stringy monster? And is each mushroom a head? No, each mushroom is more like the fingertip of an underground giant. When you put those mushrooms—not just one but the whole group of fungi above the ground—and the entire underground network together, that's the real fungal body.

A fungal thread is also called a **hypha** (high-fa). If there are two or more, they are called "hyphae" (high-fee).

The network of a single fungus is also known as a **mycelium** (my-seal-i-um)—quite a tricky word to pronounce!

On average, a human hair is 30 times as thick as a fungal thread.

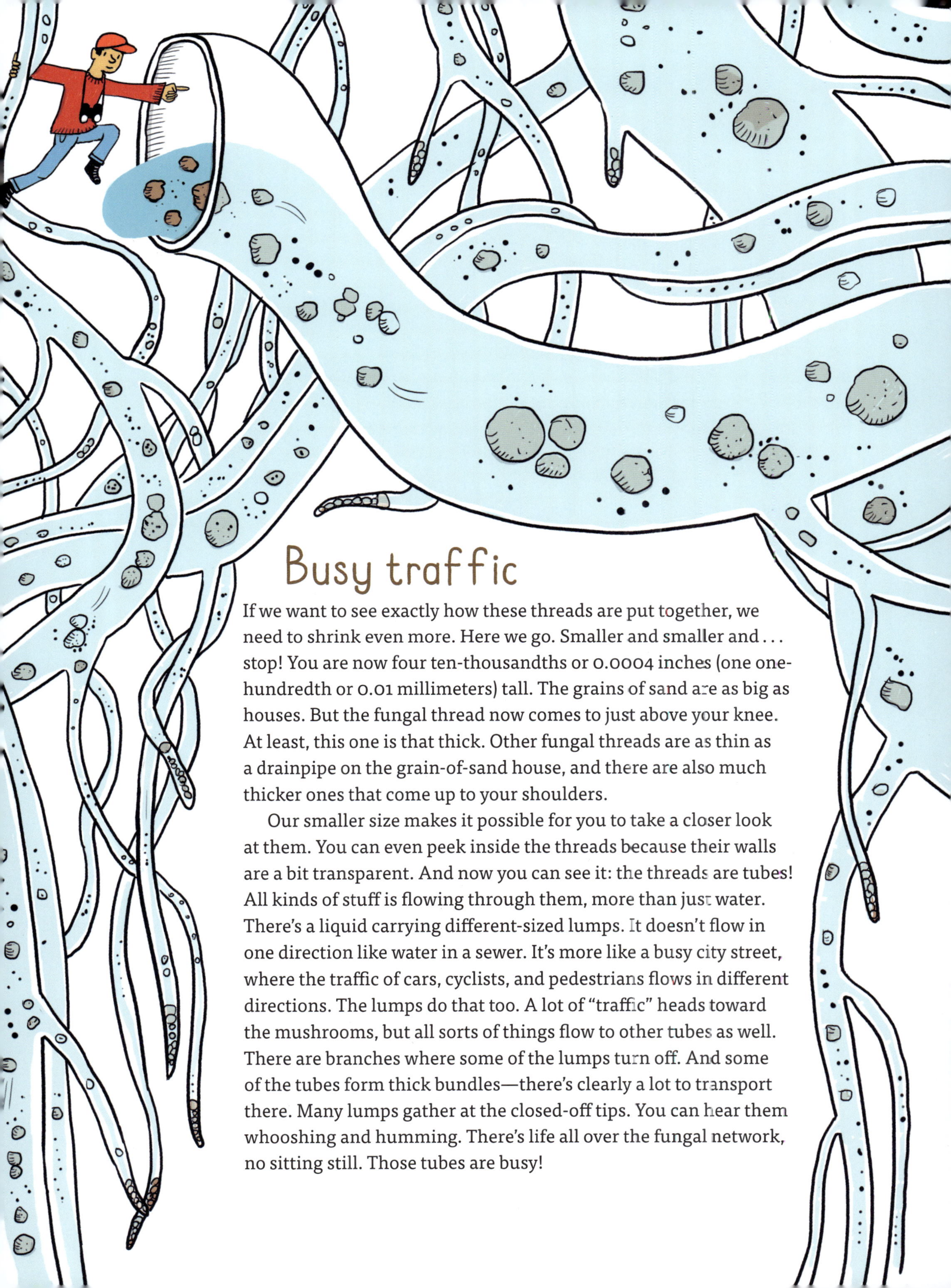

## Busy traffic

If we want to see exactly how these threads are put together, we need to shrink even more. Here we go. Smaller and smaller and . . . stop! You are now four ten-thousandths or 0.0004 inches (one one-hundredth or 0.01 millimeters) tall. The grains of sand are as big as houses. But the fungal thread now comes to just above your knee. At least, this one is that thick. Other fungal threads are as thin as a drainpipe on the grain-of-sand house, and there are also much thicker ones that come up to your shoulders.

Our smaller size makes it possible for you to take a closer look at them. You can even peek inside the threads because their walls are a bit transparent. And now you can see it: the threads are tubes! All kinds of stuff is flowing through them, more than just water. There's a liquid carrying different-sized lumps. It doesn't flow in one direction like water in a sewer. It's more like a busy city street, where the traffic of cars, cyclists, and pedestrians flows in different directions. The lumps do that too. A lot of "traffic" heads toward the mushrooms, but all sorts of things flow to other tubes as well. There are branches where some of the lumps turn off. And some of the tubes form thick bundles—there's clearly a lot to transport there. Many lumps gather at the closed-off tips. You can hear them whooshing and humming. There's life all over the fungal network, no sitting still. Those tubes are busy!

# Pieces of life

When you walk along a tube, you sometimes see a partition inside. That partition is not a closed wall. It slows down the flow, but it has openings through which the lumps can pass.
If you look through the wall of the tube, you'll see what's going on—especially if you've been taught about **cells** at school. Each part of the tube between two partitions is a cell.

Everything alive is made up of cells. Yes, even you. Cells are mainly made up of liquid. Fortunately, that liquid is enclosed in a shell, or life would be an oozy mess. Inside a fungus, those cell shells are sturdier than the ones in your body. This is because they are largely made of **chitin**. That's the same material insects, spiders, and lobsters use to make their outer covering—or exoskeleton—tough.

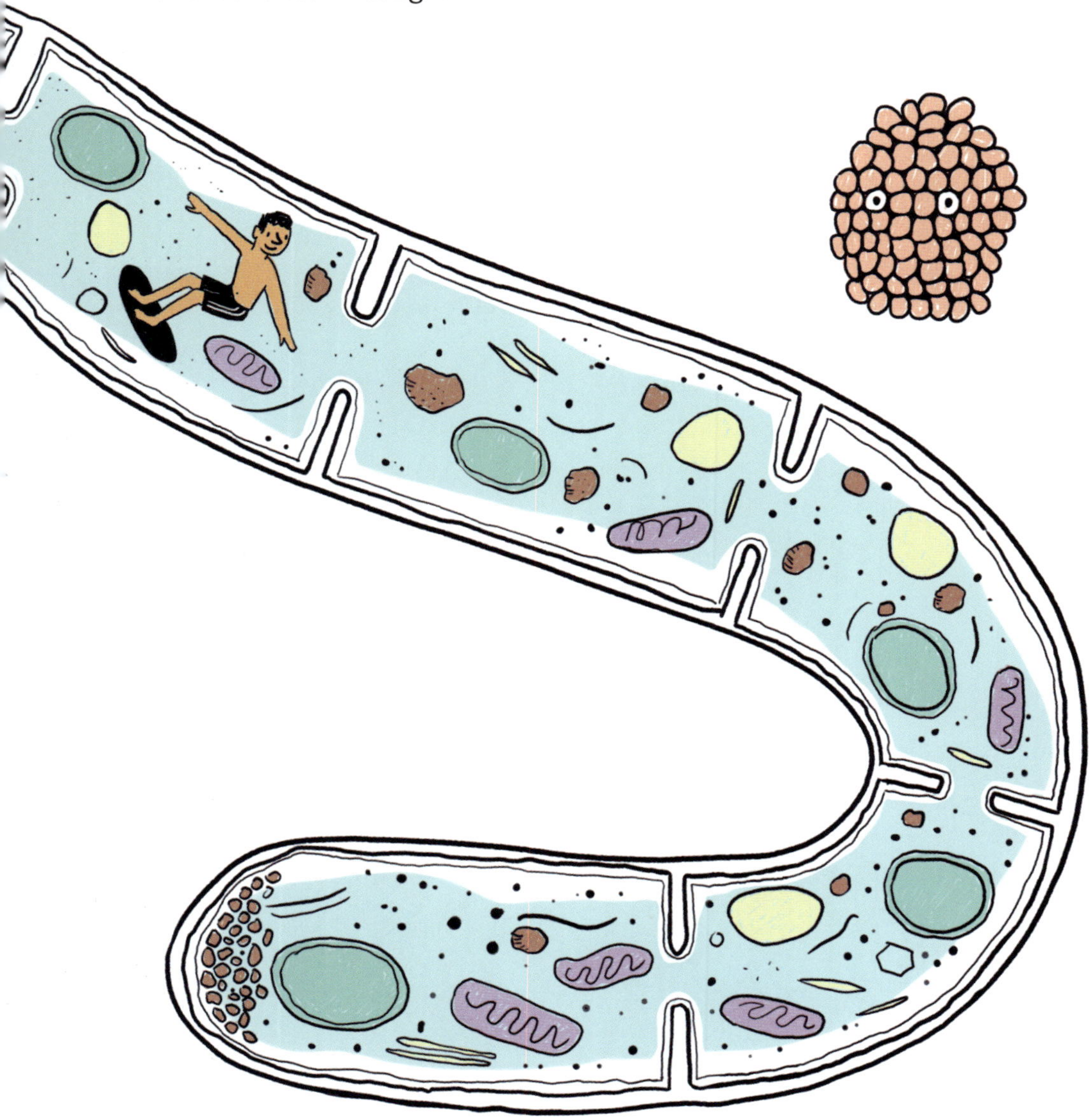

# Well organized

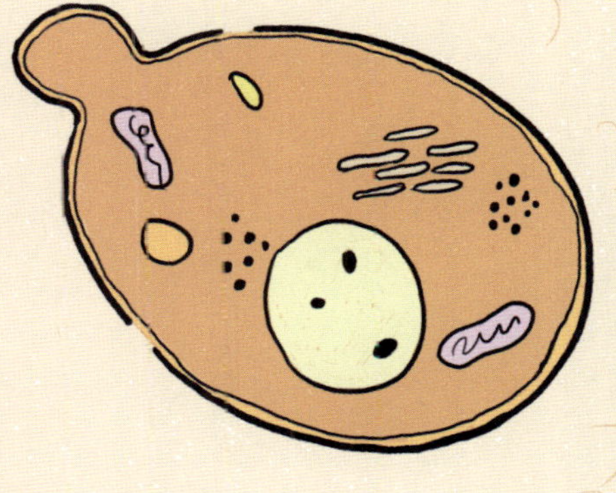

Real life is inside the cell. If you know nothing about cells, it probably just seems like a soup of balls and lumps. But a cell is definitely not a soupy mess; a cell is fantastically organized. It contains chemical factories that change substances into things the cell can use. And it even has a kind of brain to keep track of everything: the **cell nucleus**.

Cells work well together. They divvy up tasks. And so in fungi, they form long tubes and networks together. But some cells can manage life alone. A creature that consists of just one cell (and can live just fine like that) is called "unicellular." The slipper animalcule, for example, consists of only one cell. Similarly, there are single-celled fungi. These are called **yeasts**. Speaking of which, there are also yeasts under the ground here (yes, we're still there, shrunk and all). They are those balls you can see everywhere between the grain-of-sand houses. And particularly on those beams made of splinters.

A cell can grow, but not indefinitely. If it's fully grown but still wants to grow some more, a cell has to split. Then it becomes two cells. Just look at that big ball of yeast at the top right-hand side of this page: a smaller ball is growing out of it. If you wait an hour, you'll see the new yeast cell next to its mother. So there are now two yeast cells. That's how yeast reproduces. And it does this a lot! Sometimes the cell numbers double every two hours: super-speedy yeast!

**There are thousands of types of yeast. They look very similar, but often they aren't related at all.**

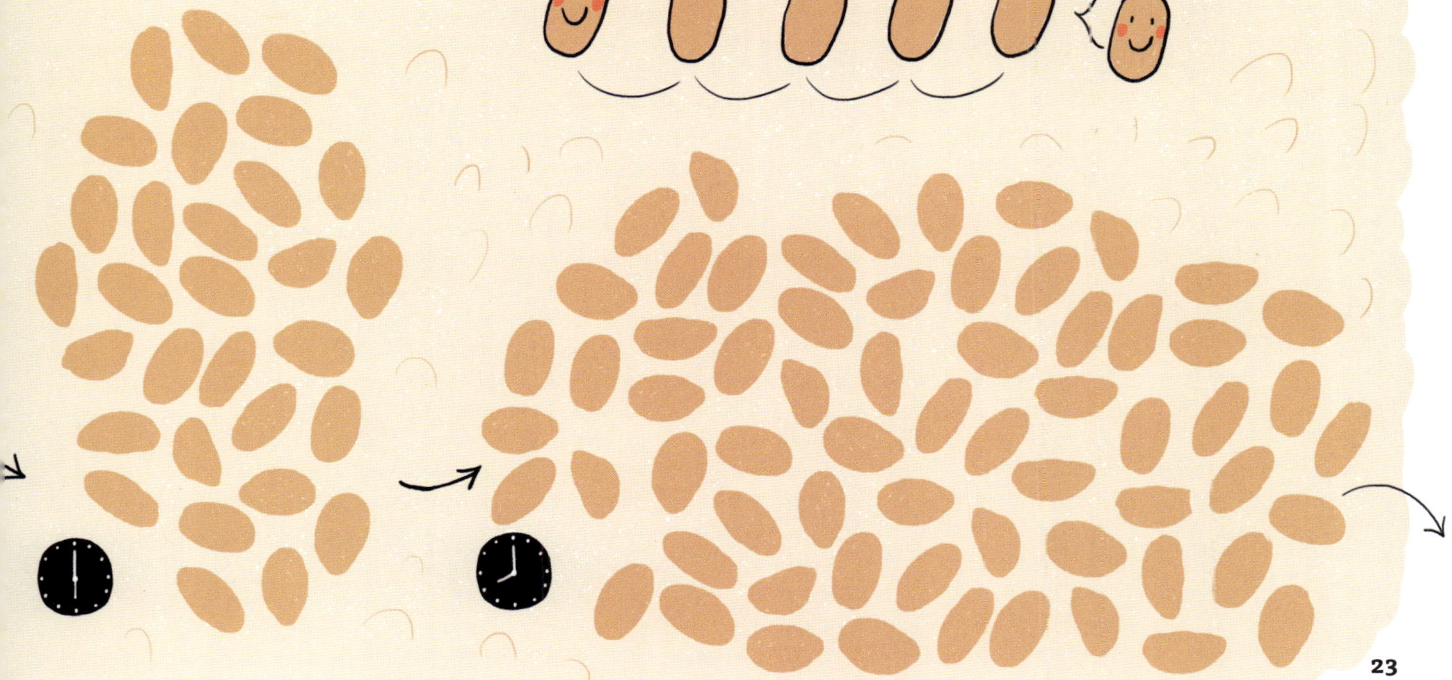

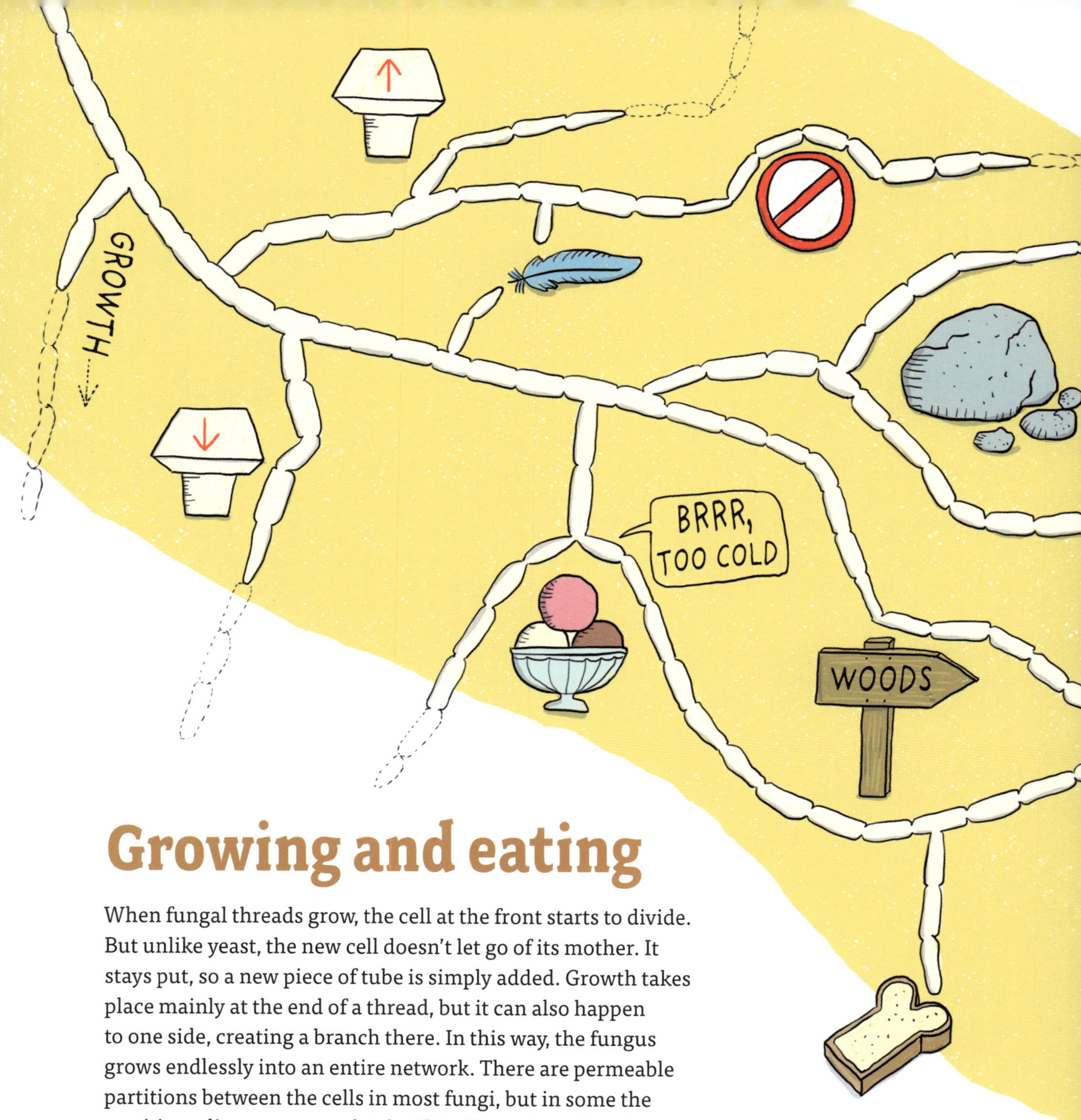


# Growing and eating

When fungal threads grow, the cell at the front starts to divide. But unlike yeast, the new cell doesn't let go of its mother. It stays put, so a new piece of tube is simply added. Growth takes place mainly at the end of a thread, but it can also happen to one side, creating a branch there. In this way, the fungus grows endlessly into an entire network. There are permeable partitions between the cells in most fungi, but in some the partitions disappear completely. This allows those fungi to act quickly. They send chemical factories and cell nuclei (the plural of "nucleus") to where they are needed the most, like a growth tip. This is how fungi are able to grow at such lightning speed.

Fungi don't just grow randomly. They head somewhere specific. In a way, fungi can observe their surroundings. They can feel gravity, for instance. This means they know exactly what is up and what is down.

**Masterminds**

**Yeasts are cleverer than other single-celled organisms because when it suits them, they can also grow into a network of more cells. This reveals their true nature: they are and remain fungi.**

# In search of food

Fungi are mainly looking for food: they can only grow if they eat well. And the opposite is also true: a fungus can only eat if it grows well. It doesn't have legs or wings, so it must grow toward its goal. Before a fungus has discovered where the food is, it grows in all directions. If a growth tip bumps up against something, it grows sideways. If it hesitates between left or right, it grows both ways, splitting into two branches. If a fungal tip tastes or smells that there is something to eat somewhere, it gets help from the other tips in the network and the fungus starts to grow more in that direction.

A growing fungal thread will not let itself be stopped without a fight. If it really wants to go somewhere, the cell right at the front pumps its tip full of water. With a force five times greater than the pressure of a bicycle tire pump, the tip can often push itself inside of the obstacle. This allows fungal threads to penetrate wood, which some fungi are fond of eating. Or a tree leaf, dead or alive. Or a human toenail.

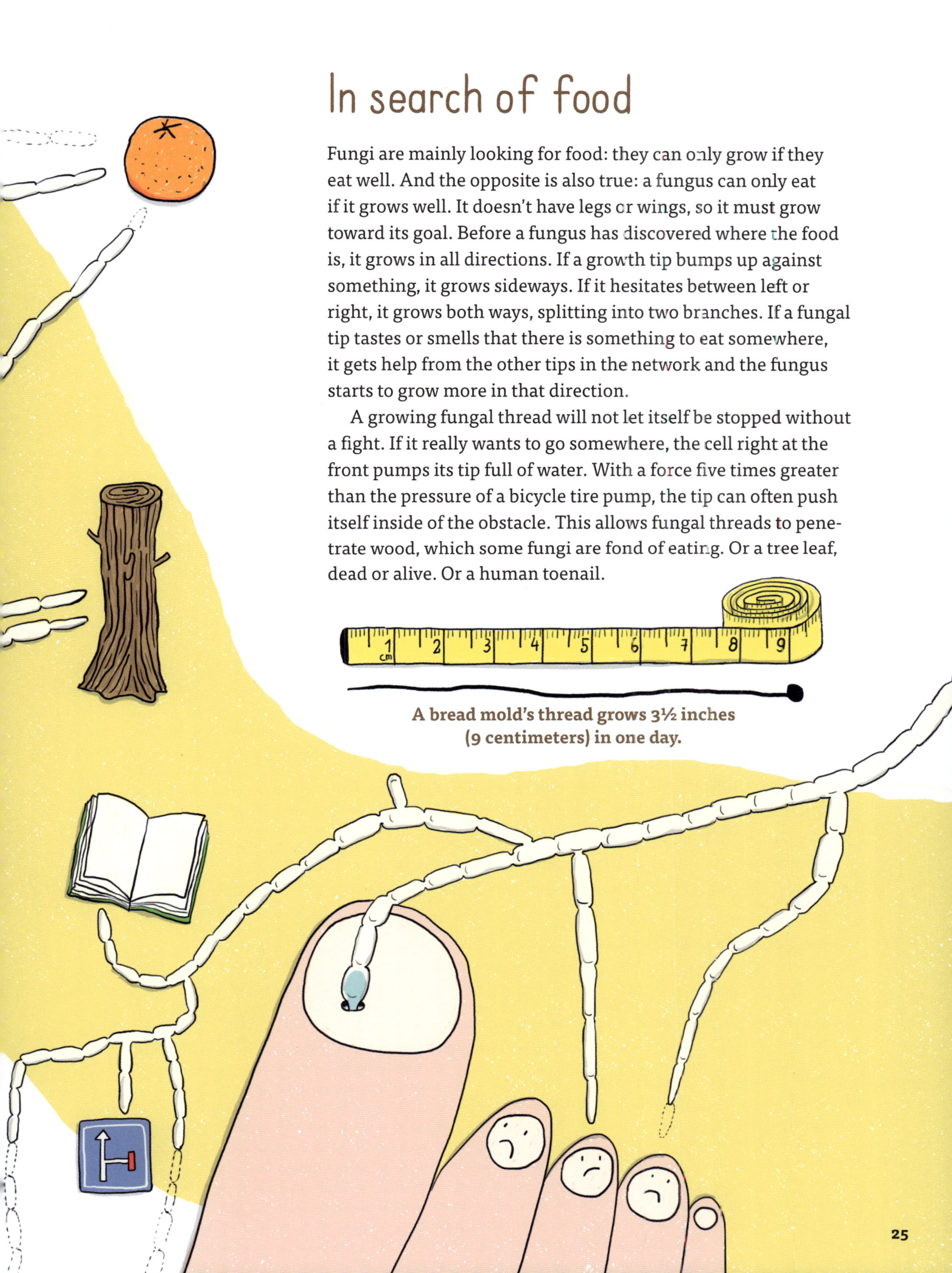


**A bread mold's thread grows 3½ inches (9 centimeters) in one day.**

# Little bites

Fungi don't have mouths, or a stomach. But they can eat, and they can digest food. We eat first and then digest; a fungus does it in reverse order. If a fungal cell tastes something edible, its tiny "brain" instructs its factories to make digestive juices. The cell then spits those juices over the food. The food is digested and the nutritious soup is taken into the cell. It is processed there to be used as energy, and to grow—basically, to live.

Not every fungus likes the same food. Different species of fungi have different preferences. These are mainly based on what they can digest. Some fungi eat the same food as we do—a slice of bread will do perfectly for a bread mold. But there are also some that can eat stuff that is indigestible for others. Feathers, for instance. And wood. The **cellulose** that all plants are filled with, living and dead. Some even manage to break down tough, woody **lignin**. A clever piece of digestion work: nothing else can do it. Once the nutrients are inside the fungal cell, the whole fungus can enjoy them. They are transported through the tubular threads to where they are needed. In the fungal threads without partitions, this happens really fast—a bit like blood flowing through blood vessels.

**Plants have a solid shell around their cells. This cell wall is made of cellulose. Our intestines find it hard to break down, but heat can help. That's why we can digest cooked vegetables much more easily than raw ones.**

**Poison-eaters**
Some fungi have strange tastes. They might like to eat aircraft fuel, for instance. Some can even grow in the chemicals used in a photo lab.

# Poop sandwich

A fungal cell also produces waste, of course. The fungus ejects it. Bread mold simply does this right where it's growing. So it doesn't just eat that sandwich bread or piece of toast, it also poops on it. Just so you know.

Sometimes a fungus has too much water in its cells. It squeezes it out. You can sometimes see drops of liquid on the dead wood on which a fungus is feasting. And sometimes on the edge of a mushroom. Many people think this is dew, but now you know better: it's fungus sweat or mushroom pee.

# When fungi meet

So far, we've only been talking about the tubular network of a single fungus. But if that network grows a lot, fungi can also run into neighboring fungi—of their own kind or a different sort. If a fungus encounters another species, it will usually stop growing there. The other also stops. They agree not to get in each other's way and make a kind of wall. With wood fungi, this is visible as a clear dark line in the wood. But sometimes they argue. The fungi attack, spitting out substances that are nasty or poisonous to the other. One fungus may even eat the other, but more about that later. A fungus is less aggressive when it meets its own kind; then they just grow through and around each other.

**These cell nuclei already live together in one cell, but are putting off fusing for now.**

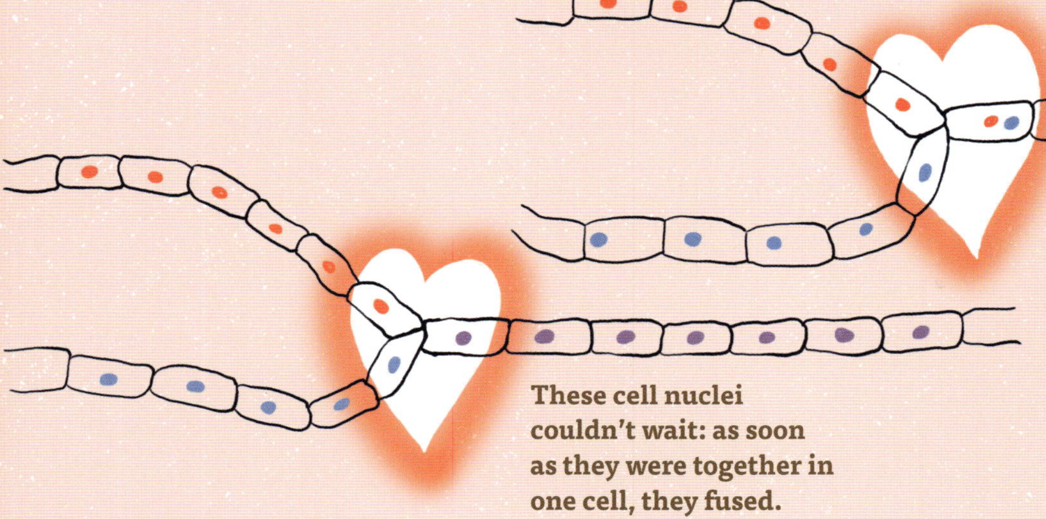

**These cell nuclei couldn't wait: as soon as they were together in one cell, they fused.**

## Fungus sex

Sometimes, while growing, fungi find one of their kind and just click. Sparks fly and they fuse together. Two cells become one. The two nuclei of those cells also fuse, but many fungi delay doing this for a while.

It looks like sex, and actually it is. In humans and other animals, fusion happens with single cells. A sperm cell fuses with an egg cell. With flowers it's the same, only you call the sperm cells "pollen." In fungi, the sex cells are simply attached to the rest of the fungal body.

**Many different genders**
In most fungi, there's not just a male and a female but many genders. To us, the difference cannot be seen, but the fungi themselves can smell it immediately. They only mate with a fungus of a different gender. In this, they have a lot of choice. Some species have as many as 28 genders!

## Making babies

1+1=1

1+1=
lots and lots

That fusion is indeed sex, because a new fungus is created. A fungus child with the characteristics of both parents. But it's not reproduction. With reproduction, you make many from just one or two. Fusion is the opposite: you turn two things into one. Of course, there still need to be children.

Fungi have a way. They can make lots of children at once. Fungi make a kind of seed, like a plant does. These seeds are really tiny fungal children, and each is only one cell in size. A fungal seed is called a **spore**.

Spores are not only to make more fungi, but also to get the fungal offspring to places where the parent fungi themselves cannot go. After all, they can only move around by growing.

# Balls and balconies

For fungi that live hidden away—in the soil or in wood, for example—now is the time to make spores in a special spore carrier. The thousands of threads of a single fungus join forces. Together, they build a fungal mass with a special shape. A stem with a hat, for example. Or a dust-filled ball. Or a little balcony on a tree trunk. If you're thinking these descriptions seem familiar, you're on the right track: these spore carriers are the mushrooms.

But there are molds that aren't as well hidden. When it's time for them to grow, they send their threads over their food. A sandwich, for example, or a rotten orange. These molds don't make mushrooms. Instead, they simply send out their spores on tiny spore carriers, which sometimes don't even have a stalk.

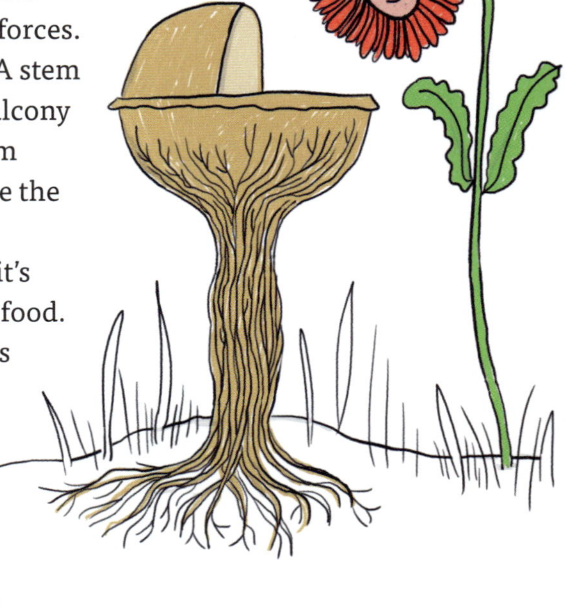


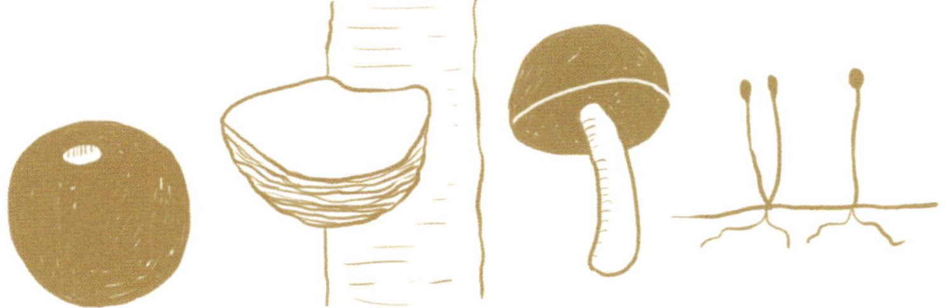

### Sexless fungi

**For fungi, sex and reproduction are often separate. Spores may arise immediately after fusion; that is, after sex. But they can also come much later, as tiny single cells. This is what happens in most fungi. Many species never even have sex, or they do it so secretly that scientists have never seen it.**

**A single moldy orange produces around 10 billion spores. That's over 2 billion more than the number of people in the entire world.**

## Nice and small

So, as we've said, spores are small. Most are not much thicker than the fungal thread from which they were formed. If we go back to our shrunken state—where a human hair is over 30 feet (10 meters) thick—the average spores would be between the size of a tennis ball and a large beach ball. Spores vary in shape from one fungal species to another. Some look like little balls or eggs, but others are elongated like mini sausages or curly like springs. Their surface might be smooth or puckered, and some spores have threads sticking out of them.

**Spores galore!**
**The number of spores a single mushroom makes is enormous. One fly agaric makes about 2 billion, while a giant puffball blasts up to 2,000 billion (2 trillion) spores into the air!**

# The big wide world

The spore's main task is to find a new home—and not right next to its mother, because that's space she needs to grow into. Instead, the spore babies have to go out into the big wide world. That's what they're designed for. Because they are so small, spores blow away easily. Many mushrooms give their spores a helping hand by releasing them a little above the ground. If the spores swirl down from the underside of the cap, they can easily be carried away by a gust of wind.

All mushrooms give their spores their first push. When the spores break loose, they are automatically pushed away. Some are literally shot into the air, at speeds of up to 375 miles per hour (600 kilometers per hour)!

# Hitchhikers

Some fungi use animals to spread their spores. They lure insects with a drop of sugary water, for example, or with the smell of poop or rotten meat. This won't attract bees or butterflies, but dung flies and bluebottles love it. A stinkhorn attracts them from a long way away. The insects walk through its sticky mass of spores, which clings to their feet, just waiting to be planted elsewhere. What a clever fungus!

**Truffles** have to work extra hard to spread their spores. This is because they grow underground. But they've got a plan. A truffle gives off a smell that wild boar, squirrels, and voles love. If these animals smell one, they will root open the ground and eat the truffle full of spores. The spores pass through their stomach and intestines without any problems and are pooped out again at another place in the forest.

Name: **cup fungus** | Scientific name: ***Cookeina speciosa***

Cup fungi make their spores on the inside of a cup. This variety, from the Amazonian rainforest, has cups on stalks. They look like wineglasses!

Name: **fluted bird's nest** | Scientific name: ***Cyathus striatus***

Often found on wood chips. Looks like a tiny cupcake wrapper covered in the fur of a shaggy bear. There are "eggs" at the bottom of the cup, just like in a bird's nest.

# Tails for swimming

Many fungi from wet environments make spores that can swim. That's right: they swim! They have tails just like tadpoles do—and yes, just like the sperm cell of an animal. But unlike a sperm cell, which needs to fertilize an egg to make reproduction happen, a swimming spore can manage just fine on its own. They can smell, so they follow their noses to a suitable habitat where they linger and grow into a fungal network. If all goes well, they reproduce there by making their own spores.

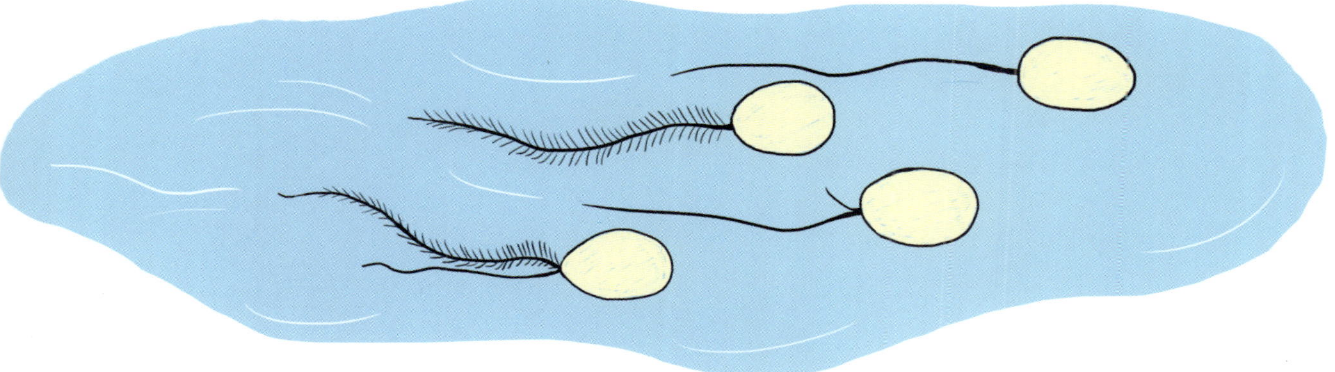

# Traveling lumps

Fungi don't spread only in spore form; they can also spread through a tuft of fungal thread. If it is small enough, a tuft can easily be carried away by the wind, by water, or by a passing animal. Sometimes a tuft of fungus breaks off by accident, but some break off on purpose. They form little lumps, survival packs with extra food and a protective jacket. These blow along a little less easily than spores, but they have a much better start.

Bird's nest fungi even make cups containing tiny spherical survival packs (called **peridioles**) that each contain a huge number of spores. If a raindrop falls into one of these cups, the survival packs are thrown upward. A thread with a sticky end dangles from the pack. It uses this to stick to a blade of grass once it lands. With a bit of luck, the pack is then eaten by a cow, which eventually poops out the spores. Smart!

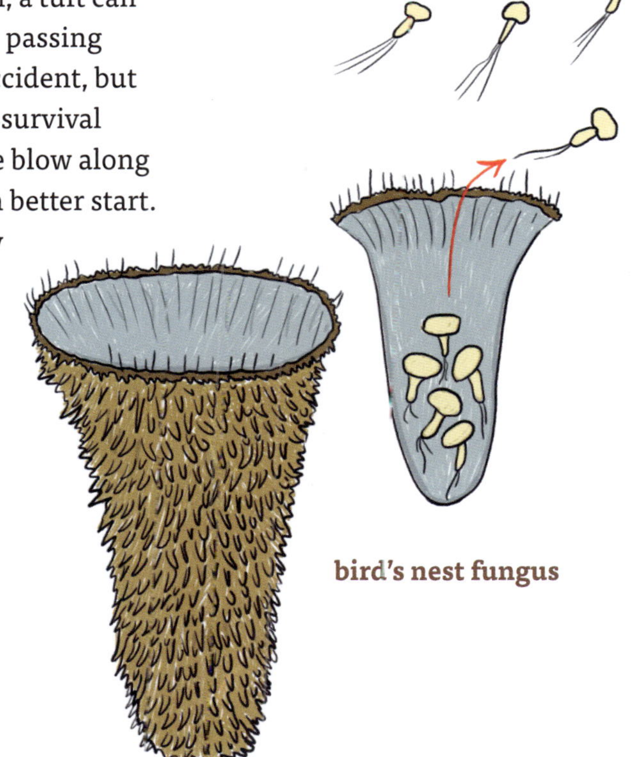

**bird's nest fungus**

# Popping up like mushrooms

A fungus, as you now know, consists of a network of fungal threads. When the fungus is ready to make mushrooms, fungal threads start knotting together. They form a compact egg just under the ground. With its flexible but tough shell, it looks a bit like a lizard's egg. And just as a baby lizard grows inside a lizard egg, a mushroom grows inside the fungal egg. The unborn mushroom is very compact and squashed, but fully formed. The only thing missing is water. Basically, it's an instant mushroom in a waterproof package.

**The egg with the instant mushroom inside is called a primordium.**

The fungus waits for the right moment. A wet autumn night, for example. Then the fungal network drinks a lot and pumps water into the egg. The squashed mushroom swells, the eggshell bursts open, the stem stretches, the cap unfolds, and—ta-da! A complete mushroom! It seems like magic, and people used to think it was.

**From left to right, you can see how a fly agaric emerges from its egg. Within a few days it's perfect—fully grown and unfolded, with all the trimmings. Then it does what it was built to do: it spreads spores.**

# Under the hood

A standard mushroom consists of a stalk and a cap. Sometimes there are remnants of the "eggshell": a ring around the stalk, a few shreds on the cap. The real work happens under the cap, where the mushroom makes its spores. To do this, it needs a lot of space there. Many mushrooms create this space by making hanging flaps, called **gills**. They look a bit like the gills of a fish. The gills create a lot of surface area, like the pages of a book. The spores are made on the walls of these flaps. When they are released, they swirl down between the gills.

CAP
GILLS
SPORES
RING
STALK
(also called a STIPE)
BASE

## Four models

Mushrooms with flaps under their caps are called **agarics**. There are also mushrooms that make their spores on the inner wall of tubes (**tube fungi**) or on the outside of hanging spikes (**tooth fungi**). And then you have mushrooms that make spores inside their round bellies. Only when they are ripe do these **puffball mushrooms** burst open, ejecting their spores.

- The poisonous fly agaric is the most famous agaric.
- The king bolete or "penny bun" is a tube fungus.
- The pig's trotter is a tooth fungus.
- The earthball is a puffball mushroom.

earthball

pig's trotter

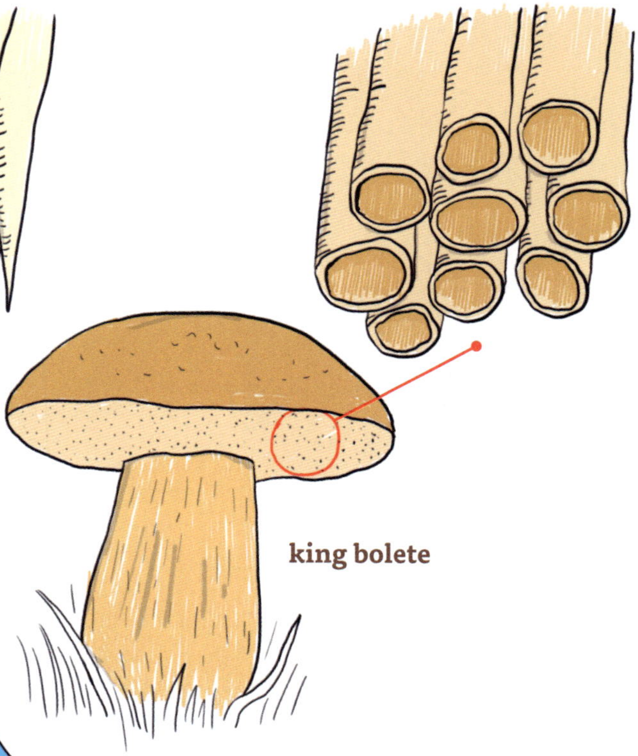

king bolete

fly agaric

Tube fungi with very tight tubes are called **sponge fungi.** And puffballs are also called **gasteroid fungi.**

# Powerhouses

You know what a mushroom feels like: sort of like a hard-boiled egg. Pretty firm, in other words. But they are easy to cut. Nevertheless, it's amazing how strong mushrooms and other fungi are. When they pop up out of the ground, they're not stopped by a layer of pine needles or soil. Pavement mushrooms sometimes lift paving stones, and inkcaps can even break through asphalt.

Some fungus is rock hard—the birch polypore, for example. It only has a cap, or rather half a cap, growing from the trunk of a birch tree. But this fungus is almost as sturdy as the wood of that tree. The hoof fungus, which often grows on beech trees, also looks like it is made of beech wood. If you knock on it, this chunky mushroom sounds just like a block of wood.

Leathery or woody mushrooms can live for a few years. Softer mushrooms decay quickly. A week is relatively long; some last only a few days. Many autumn fungi can't handle frost. If the temperature has been well below 32 degrees Fahrenheit (0 degrees Celsius) at night, they turn into a soggy mess the next day. This is sad to see, but for the fungus it doesn't matter. Its spores have already been dispersed. Mission accomplished.

pavement mushroom

# The Super Fungus grid

When its mushrooms are dead, the fungus lives on, just as an oak tree does after dropping its acorns. How long a fungus lives is variable. Some live for only a year; others are still growing like fresh young fungi centuries later. You can sometimes tell from the mushrooms on the ground how old the fungus is underground. Here's the thing: When a fungus can grow freely, its network grows in all directions. The fungus forms a disk shape under the ground. The growing tips of the fungal threads are on the outside, in a circle. The fungus mainly forms mushrooms at its tips, so the mushrooms of one fungal network stand in a neat circle. People used to think that witches or fairies had danced on that spot. Now we know better, but a circle of mushrooms is still called a "witch's circle" in countries with Germanic languages. In English, we call it a **fairy ring**.

The mushrooms disappear, but the fungus grows on. A healthy fungus that has enough to eat expands by about 3 feet (1 meter) each year—meaning the mushrooms pop up in a larger circle year after year. The older the fungus, the bigger the circle. In North America, aerial photographs showed a fairy ring over half a mile (over a kilometer) wide. That fungus is at least 1,000 years old!

# Survival capsule

Whether fungi can survive in a place depends on several things. There has to be something to eat, of course, but the temperature and humidity are also important. Many fungi like it to be warm and humid. A half-full organic waste bin in summer will fill with mold in a day. But if it's hotter than about 95 degrees Fahrenheit (35 degrees Celsius), most molds cannot cope. Inside our bodies, the temperature is about 98 degrees Fahrenheit (37 degrees Celsius). As a result, they don't last long in there, thankfully. But they can live between our toes in a damp sock.

Most fungi survive the cold well, although they don't grow much. That's why food in the fridge doesn't go moldy as quickly as food on the counter, and why it doesn't go moldy at all in the freezer. Yet fungi do live around the South Pole. They grow as soon as the temperature creeps above freezing and spend the rest of the time in a kind of hibernation. Some fungi make survival capsules with a hard outer shell, usually the size of a hazelnut. They can survive tough conditions and last for years inside them.

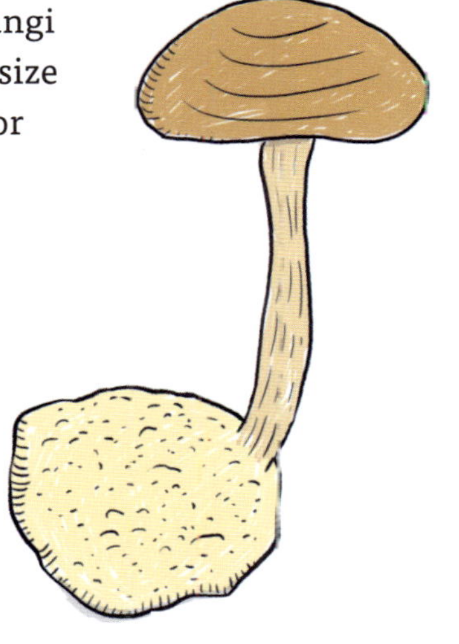

Some spores can also be quite resilient. They can blow halfway around the world and there is still life in them. They also swirl through every house and kitchen. If something can go moldy, it will.

**A fungus's survival capsule is called a sclerotium (scle-row-she-um). If there are two or more, they are called "sclerotia."**

Well, that was quite a trip through the moldy underworld! Time to grow back to human size and get yourself ready for some time travel.

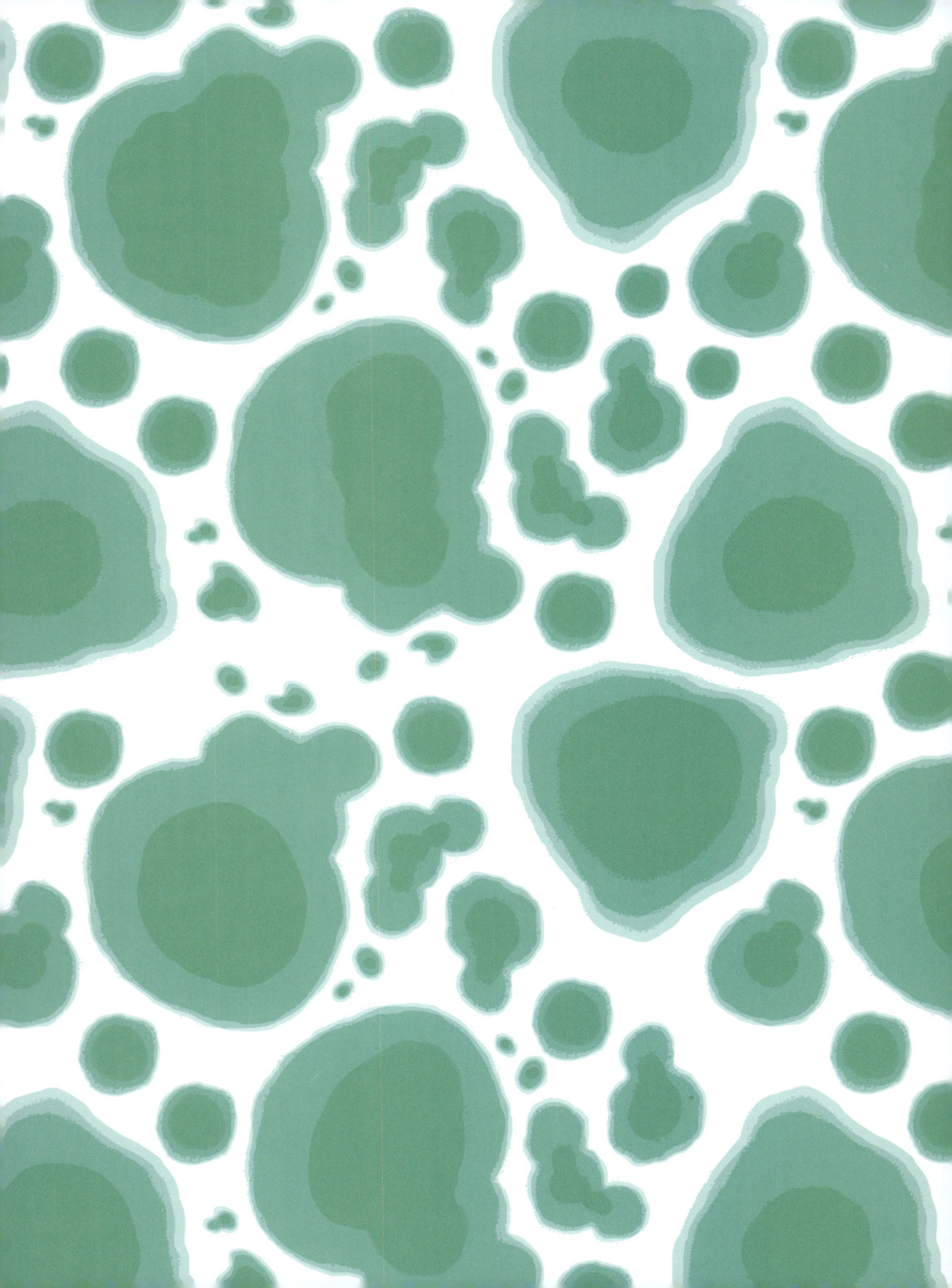

# 3 THE KINGDOM OF FUNGI

You know quite a bit about fungi now, but you don't know the most important thing—at least not yet. What *is* a fungus? Is it a plant? An animal? Both? Or neither? Not all fungi are the same. Is the orange peel fungus related to orange mold? And when did the first fungi come into existence?

# Creating order

Let's start with that first question: What is a fungus? Carl Linnaeus thought he knew. Fungi are plants, this Swedish biologist wrote in 1735 in his survey of all living things. But not a single biologist would agree with him today. After Linnaeus's death, it was discovered that plants have **chlorophyll**. This special ingredient allows them to grow using sunlight and carbon dioxide, making oxygen in the process.

Fungi can't do this. They need something more solid to eat or they won't grow. And they use up oxygen rather than producing it. In that respect, they are actually quite similar to animals. Well, they can't walk or fly, and they don't have eyes, but the same can be said about a mussel, a barnacle, or an earthworm. And chitin, the stuff fungi use to strengthen the outside of their cells, is exactly the same thing that insects, spiders, and crustaceans like shrimp or crabs use to strengthen their exoskeletons. This makes a fungus more animal than vegetable. However, if you study them closely—the way they live, how they are built—if you look with a microscope . . . well, there are just too many differences. That's why fungi were never allowed into the animal kingdom. And they are not part of the plant kingdom either because of their lack of chlorophyll.

In 1969, the English biologist Robert H. Whittaker made a survey of everything living, just like Linnaeus had done more than two centuries earlier. It was a good year for fungi, because Whittaker mentioned a third realm besides the plant and animal kingdoms: the kingdom of fungi.

And oh yes, two more kingdoms: bacteria and protists (things like protozoans and algae, which are neither plant nor animal). Five kingdoms in all, then. After that, things certainly changed. Biologists don't sit still. Unfortunately, the more they know, the more confusing and unclear things can get.

## Reasonable doubts

Science is about having doubts. It's about wanting to understand things. Scientists are curious "skeptics," or doubters. It's not surprising they keep doubting what is already known. When a new discovery is made, sometimes things turn out to be wrong. After 1969, several more changes were made to the table of everything alive. To be honest, it hasn't become any clearer. Biologists often disagree with each other. So in this book we'll keep it a bit old-fashioned. Five kingdoms: plant kingdom, animal kingdom, fungal kingdom, and the two other kingdoms. Hooray for the kingdom of fungi!

# A fungal history

Fungi have been around for a long time, but they weren't the first living things. Earth has existed for 4.5 billion years, and about 4 billion years ago, the first life appeared: bacteria in the ocean. The earth itself was then only half a billion years old and had barely cooled down. Then, 3.5 billion years ago, algae appeared. These tiny plant-like organisms that live in seawater released oxygen in the water and into the air. Life went on developing and all kinds of things happened. The sea became filled with living bacteria and algae, and the seafloor became covered in dead algae that bacteria feasted on. But the bacteria couldn't digest all of the algae. So a lot of gunk piled up. Much of the dead-algae sludge ended up under the ground and is still there today. We know it as petroleum, the source of oil and gas.

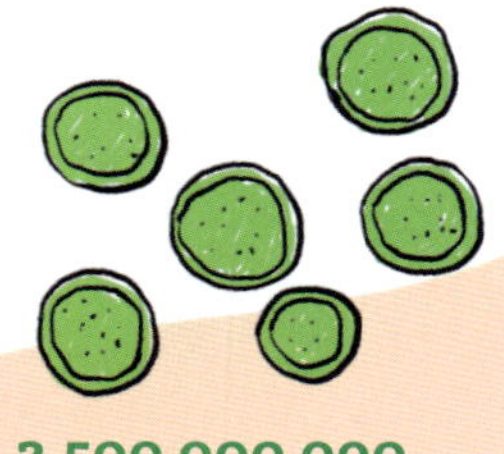

**2,400,000,000 years ago**
first fungi

**3,500,000,000 years ago**
first algae

**4,000,000,000 years ago**
first life (bacteria)

## Beastly fungus child

About 2.4 billion years ago, bacteria were joined by stringy creatures that were even better at digesting dead algae. That's right: fungi! But what about animals? Well, you might be disappointed to learn that they only came into existence about 700 million years ago. They evolved from a fungus that behaved more like an animal than a fungus. Which is why fungi and animals are more alike than fungi and plants. They both have chitin, remember? And their eating habits are similar. Since we are also animals, you're more closely related to a mushroom than a dandelion!

**4,500,000,000 years ago**
Earth was formed

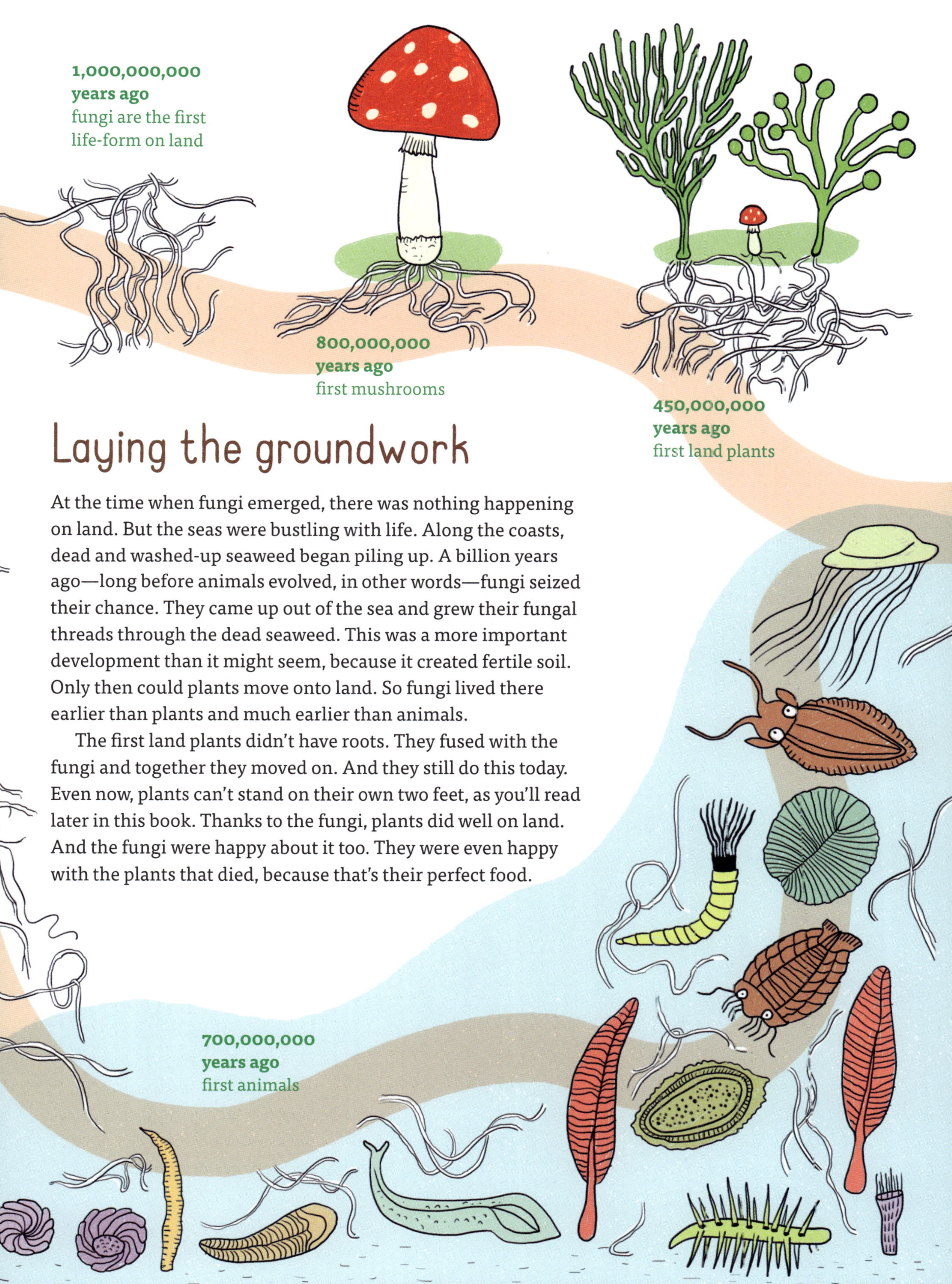


# Laying the groundwork

At the time when fungi emerged, there was nothing happening on land. But the seas were bustling with life. Along the coasts, dead and washed-up seaweed began piling up. A billion years ago—long before animals evolved, in other words—fungi seized their chance. They came up out of the sea and grew their fungal threads through the dead seaweed. This was a more important development than it might seem, because it created fertile soil. Only then could plants move onto land. So fungi lived there earlier than plants and much earlier than animals.

The first land plants didn't have roots. They fused with the fungi and together they moved on. And they still do this today. Even now, plants can't stand on their own two feet, as you'll read later in this book. Thanks to the fungi, plants did well on land. And the fungi were happy about it too. They were even happy with the plants that died, because that's their perfect food.

# A woody mess

But 360 million years ago, things went wrong. The plants started becoming trees, and they invented wood, full of cellulose and lignin, so that they'd be stronger. Today some fungi would lick their lips at that, but those new-to-land fungi had a problem. The early trees made a mess of things. Dead trees just piled up on the ground. Heaps of old wood ended up under the ground and got pressed together. That old wood is still in the ground in many places. It resembles black stone, but like wood, it is still combustible. We know it as coal. Fortunately, fungi eventually got the hang of things: 300 million years ago, they learned to digest wood.

**425,000,000 years ago**
first land animals (millipedes)

**360,000,000 years ago**
first trees and forests

**400,000,000 years ago**
first giant fungi called *Prototaxites*

**Ancient fungal forests**

For a long time, fungi were the largest living land creatures. About 400 million years ago, the prehistoric fungus *Prototaxites* grew in columns more than 3 feet (1 meter) thick and almost 30 feet (10 meters) high. This fungal tree was much larger than the largest land plants of the time.

YUMMY!
300,000,000
years ago
first fungi that could digest wood
HI
230,000,000
years ago
first dinosaurs
BYE
66,000,000
years ago
last dinosaurs
300,000
years ago
first humans
5
1735
Linnaeus puts fungi in the plant kingdom
1969
Whittaker gives fungi their own kingdom
2025
first printing of *Mushrooms and Company*

# All the fungi at a glance

Since the emergence of early life, more and more different species have evolved. Within each kingdom, biologists divide species into broad groups known as "phyla" (fy-la; a single one is called a "phylum"). These groups are then divided into smaller and smaller groups until you get to a species.

You probably know a few phyla from the animal kingdom. Mollusks and vertebrates, for example. Those of the fungal kingdom are less well known. Fungi are also more difficult to classify into groups than plants and animals. Scientists are constantly working at it. In this book, we're assuming there are eight phyla. When you see their complicated names, you might expect a lot from them. You'd be disappointed. Five of them consist of only tiny fungi, most of them single-celled. And in some of those groups, all the species live underwater. Only the species from two phyla can be seen without much effort. These are mainly the **sac fungi** and **club fungi**—which are also known as "higher fungi." They both produce real mushrooms, which makes it easy to talk about and study them. But even in those phyla, there are a lot of dwarf species.

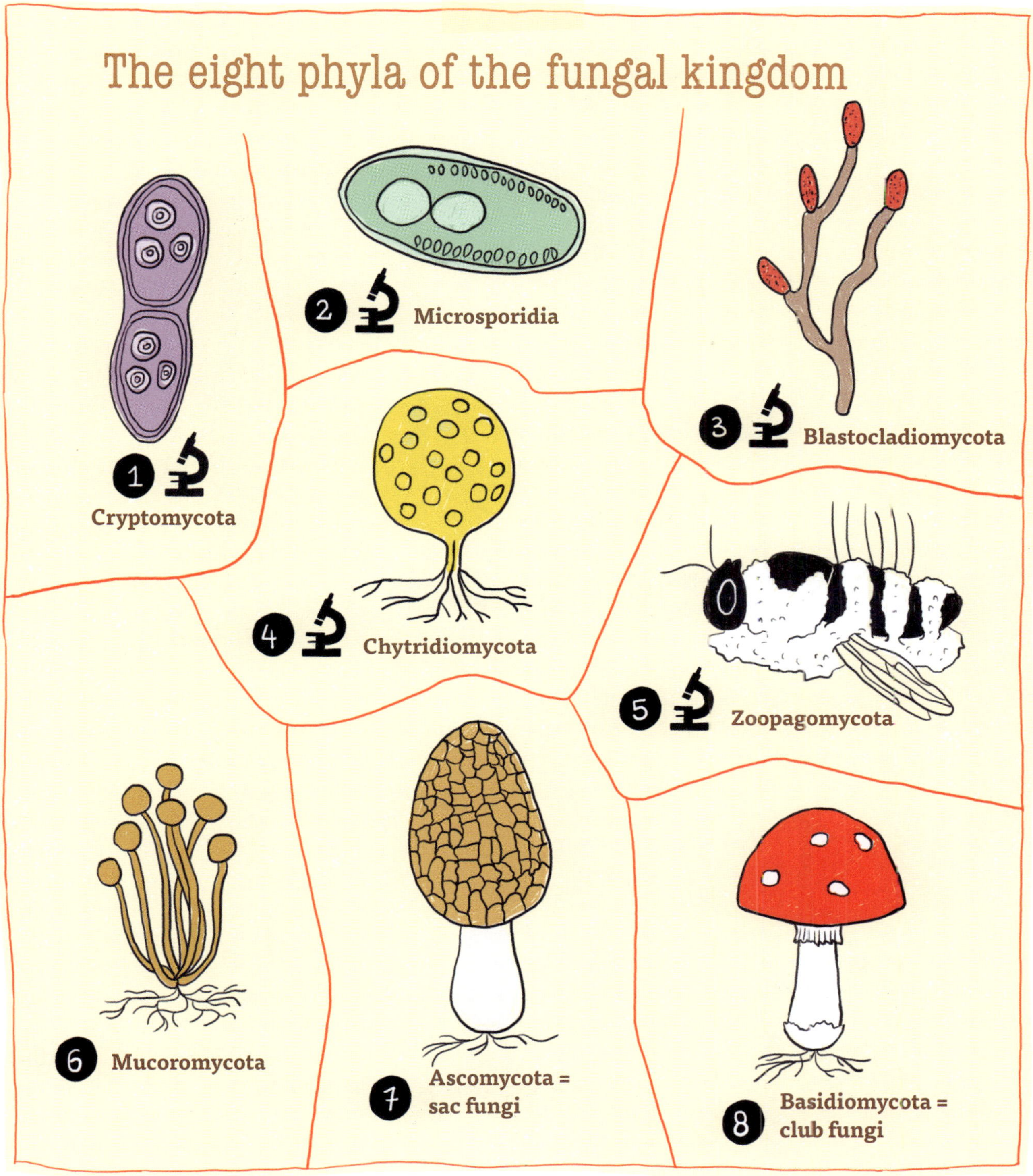
The eight phyla of the fungal kingdom
1 Cryptomycota
2 Microsporidia
3 Blastocladiomycota
4 Chytridiomycota
5 Zoopagomycota
6 Mucoromycota
7 Ascomycota = sac fungi
8 Basidiomycota = club fungi

BA-SID-EE-OH-MY-CO-TA

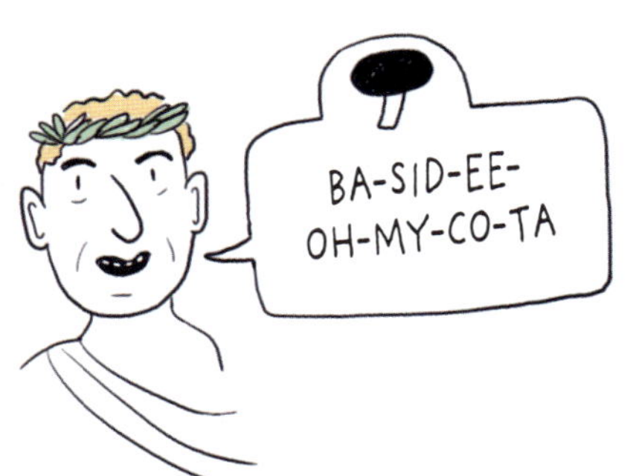

### Tongue twisters

The phyla and many species of the fungal kingdom have complicated names. They aren't easy to read and are even harder to pronounce. They are scientific names: a mishmash of Ancient Greek and Latin. Fungi that produce mushrooms are more likely to have common names.

# Mushroom makers

Sac fungi and club fungi are the real mushroom makers. *Sac fungus, club fungus*. You might think those names come from the shape of the mushroom: mushrooms like a sac and mushrooms with a kind of club. You'd be wrong. Scientists came up with the names when they started comparing the two different groups under a microscope.

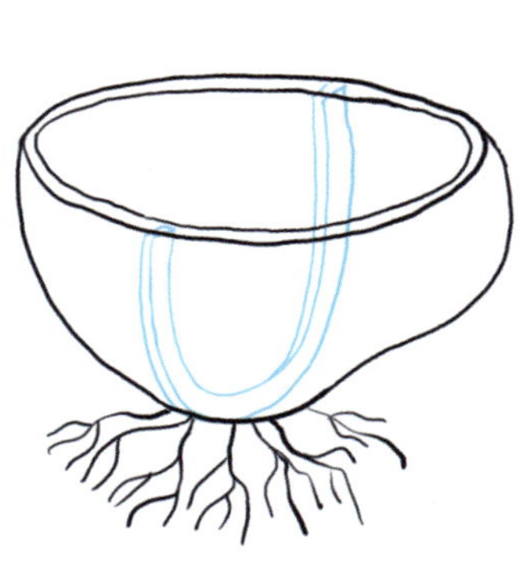

**sac fungus**

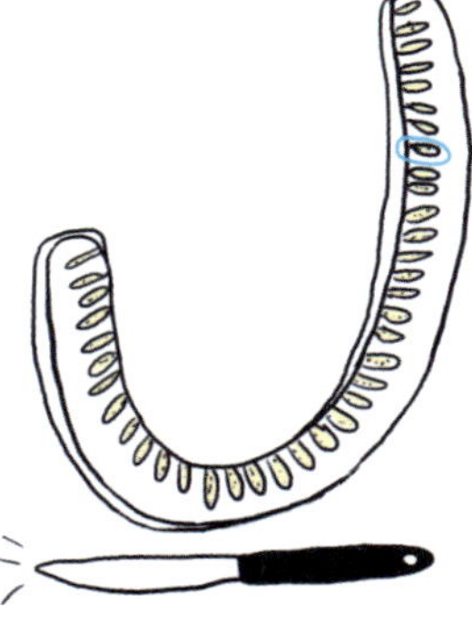

**sacs in the walls**

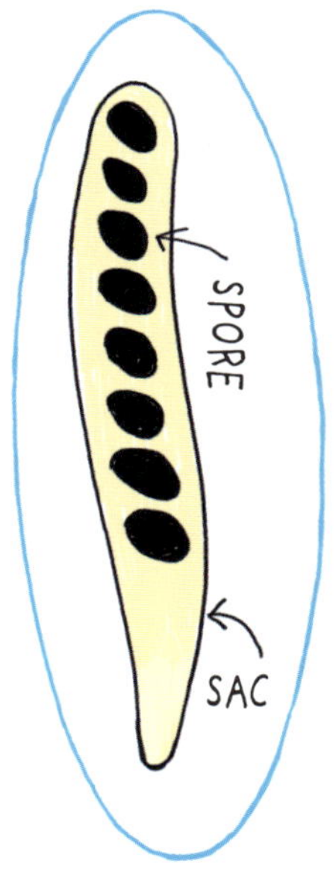


**spores in a little sac**

• With *sac fungi*, the spores are formed in elongated pouches, usually eight at a time. These spores are then neatly lined up in a row, waiting their turn until the top of the sac pops open and they are shot out.

• With *club fungi*, the spores grow on clubs sticking out of the mother cell. There are usually four of them, each on its own little club, until the club breaks and the spores are blasted out into the world.

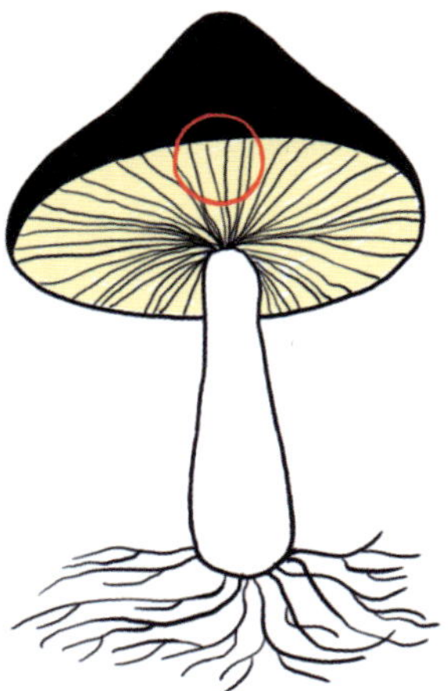

**gills under a club fungus's cap**

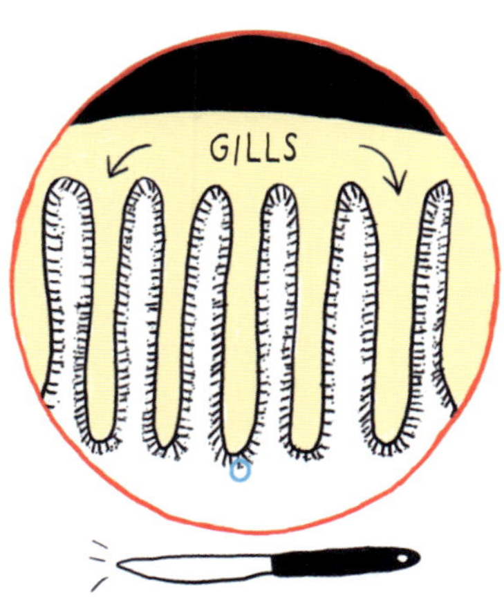


**each gill is covered in mother cells**

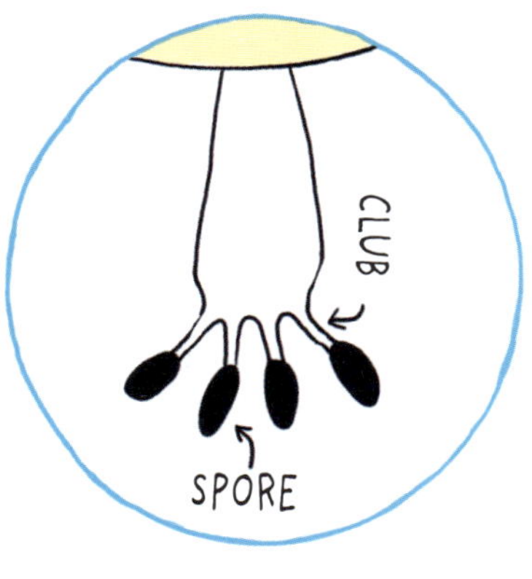


**mother cell with spores on clubs**

common morel
velvety earth tongue
white saddle
stag's horn fungus
sac fungi
orange peel fungus
large stinkhorn
turkey tail
parasol mushroom
club fungi
scarletina bolete
earthball

Name: **common morel** | Scientific name: ***Morchella esculenta***

A strange springtime mushroom, this one. Its cap looks like a maze, or a brain. Or a sponge, which is why it's also called a "sponge morel" sometimes. It doesn't look much like a cap!

# More species, fewer species

We don't actually know how many species of fungus there are. What we do know is how many have been described by biologists and given a scientific name: around 150,000. Yes, that's a lot—almost 15 times the number of bird species, to be exact. Birds are easier to spot than fungi and have been studied for a long time. Nowadays, it's rare to discover a new bird species, but with fungi it's different. Most of them are small and hidden away.

Some fungi look alike but on closer examination turn out to be different. So a new species is discovered—not really new to the world, but new to us. And another complicated name is added to the list. There are lots more species of fungi than we currently know of. Many fungal biologists think there are 2 million, but others estimate the number at 5 million or more.

And sometimes, there is suddenly one species fewer. Not because a species goes extinct but because of better research. This often happens with yeasts—which are single-celled fungi, remember? A researcher may see a yeast grow into fungal threads, and then into a network from which spore carriers eventually grow, and sometimes even into a real mushroom. The chances are this is a fungus that was already recorded under another name.

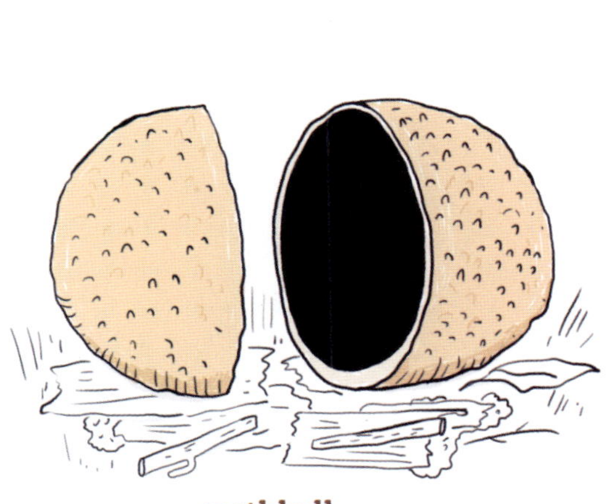

**earthball**

**fairy inkcap**

# Fake fungi

dog vomit slime mold

And then there are two groups of fake fungi: slime molds and water molds (or "oomycetes"). When you hear their names, you think: they belong. When you see them, you probably think the same thing. This is especially true of the slime molds, which you may have seen yourself in a forest. Dog vomit slime mold is a common species. The slime mold forms a large, firm yellow blob on branches. But if you stare at it for a while, you'll see something crazy. The blob moves! Is it an animal, then? It looks a bit like one. Slime molds are actually a collection of single-celled animals. Most of the time, they live separately in the soil, only occasionally clumping together into a kind of alien. Slime molds belong to one of those two other kingdoms we mentioned earlier.

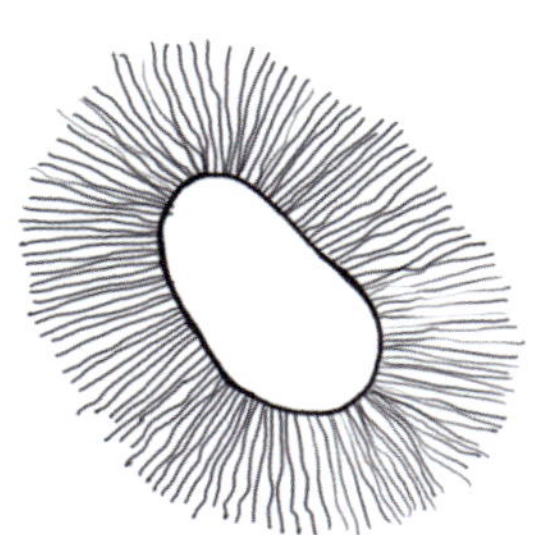

Water molds have also been kicked out of the fungal kingdom and given a place in one of those realms with the leftover small stuff. You probably don't know about water molds, unless you happen to be a potato farmer. In fact, not all of them live in water; some species live in plants. One of these is *Phytophthora* (fy-tof-thora): it lives in potato plants and kills them. The water mold rots potatoes under the ground. Potato farmers don't like *Phytophthora* very much.

So water molds and slime molds are fake fungi. But *Mushrooms and Company* isn't super strict, so we'll let them join in—if only because slime molds sometimes also make a kind of mushroom.

Whew! You've learned a lot so far. You've learned that fungi form an ancient kingdom. You know who belongs and who doesn't and that there are some tricky cases among them. Now it's time to see what all these thousands of species of fungi are up to in nature.

Name: **giant puffball** | Scientific name: ***Calvatia gigantea***

A puffball the size of a soccer ball and sometimes even bigger. Seen from late summer to autumn. Also in fields and parks. Starts off white, turns brown, and then shoots out billions of spores.

# 4 FROM RUBBISH COLLECTOR TO RAINMAKER

Fungi don't live on their own. They live with plants and animals, not to mention bacteria and other fungi. Sometimes, they make good neighbors, but other times, not so much. Survival is their main concern, and if this comes at the expense of another, so be it. But despite the fact that there are sometimes casualties, fungi have made themselves indispensable in nature.

# Dead matter



Without fungi, the world would quite literally be a mess. Let's start with the countryside. Think about a forest. Lots of things live there—so lots of things die there too. Many trees drop their leaves onto the ground in the autumn. It doesn't bother the trees: a dying leaf is no use to them. So off it goes. You'd think that all kinds of animals are hanging around, ready to clean up the mess. But you'd be wrong.

## Natural-born cleaners

Dead leaves are tough and full of lignin and cellulose. Animals can't do much with them. Fortunately, fungi can: they are natural-born cleaners. Of course, it's not that fungi are particularly neat and tidy, but they do want to eat. They love cellulose and lignin and eat it all year round, but in autumn the fungi have a real feast. That makes sense, what with all those dead leaves and the damp weather. You see the most mushrooms then. Pine needles are even more difficult to digest than regular dead leaves. So in a pine forest, you'll often see a thick layer of dead needles. But eventually, the fungi will get those too.

**The pinecone cap only likes pine cones, of course.**

# Leftovers

Many animals eat plants, but they don't digest them very well. For a fungus, there's plenty left to eat in the droppings of herbivores (plant-eaters). So fungi clean up the poop. That's nice of them. Often, a type of fungus has its own tastes. For example, some species of *Ascobolus* love deer droppings and don't like rabbit droppings, while other species of *Ascobolus* like rabbit droppings and are disgusted by deer poop.

You come across fewer dead animals in nature than you might expect. All animals die, and they don't get buried. So where do they go? If you were to wait near an animal that has just died, you'd discover the answer. Animals soon come to the body—a few foxes and crows, but mainly flies and beetles, eager for a nutritious meal. The flies lay their eggs in the dead animal and their children—maggots—eat the flesh. But animals can't really digest fur, feathers, or hooves. That's what fungi are for. If cleanup duty gets too difficult for others, they take care of it.

**Poop patrol**

**If a dog's owner doesn't clean up its poop, a common pinmold eventually will. Hopefully you haven't stepped in it first!**

**common pinmold**

***Ascobolus saccharifereus***

# Woodworkers

Poop, dead leaves, dead animals—it's nice that fungi clean them up. But what they like most of all is wood. That's not so great when the wood is a beam in your house, but fungi are really useful for forests. Dead branches regularly fall from trees, and without anyone to clean them up you'd be left with an enormous pile of branches. And even though trees can get quite old, they all die at some point, and eventually you want to get rid of them. Not just because they clog up the forest, but also because the wood contains nutrients that living trees want. So it's good for the forest that there are fungi.

Even for fungi, breaking down wood is a specialized activity. Some are better at it than others. Some prefer spruce, others beech. Which explains why you see different mushrooms appearing on a dead spruce than on a fallen beech.

**sulfur shelf**

**sulfur tuft**

**hoof fungus**

**birch polypore**

In the case of **brown rot,** the wood fungus digests only the cellulose. The rotten wood becomes crumbly and brown. With **white rot,** the wood fungus digests mainly the lignin. The rotten wood is soft and pale. Birch polypore and sulfur shelf are brown rot fungi; hoof fungus, honey fungus, and sulfur tuft are the white rot variant.

**honey fungus**

Name: **hoof fungus** | Scientific name: ***Fomes fomentarius***

Hoof fungus is a tough wood fungus. It's so hard that it even looks like it's made of wood. It mainly grows on birch and beech trees and resembles a horse's hoof. It sheds white spores in the spring, often onto its downstairs neighbors.

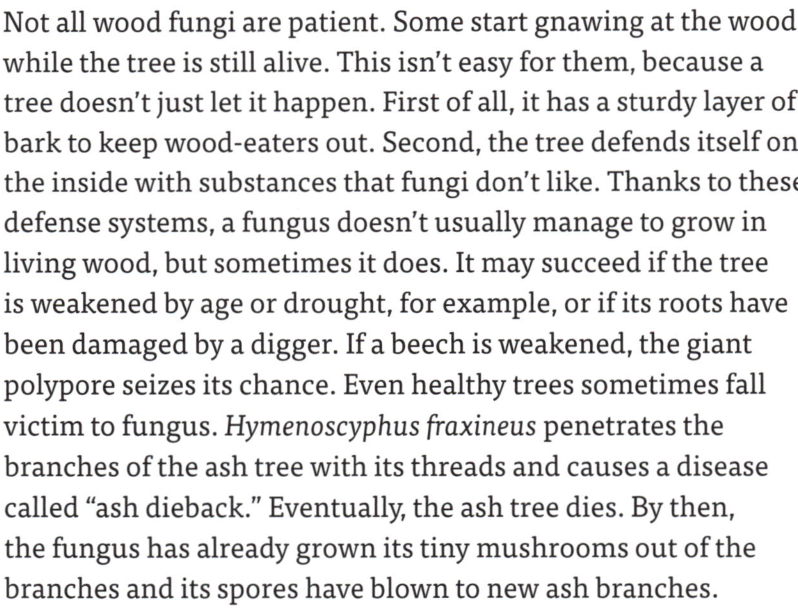


# Vegan to go

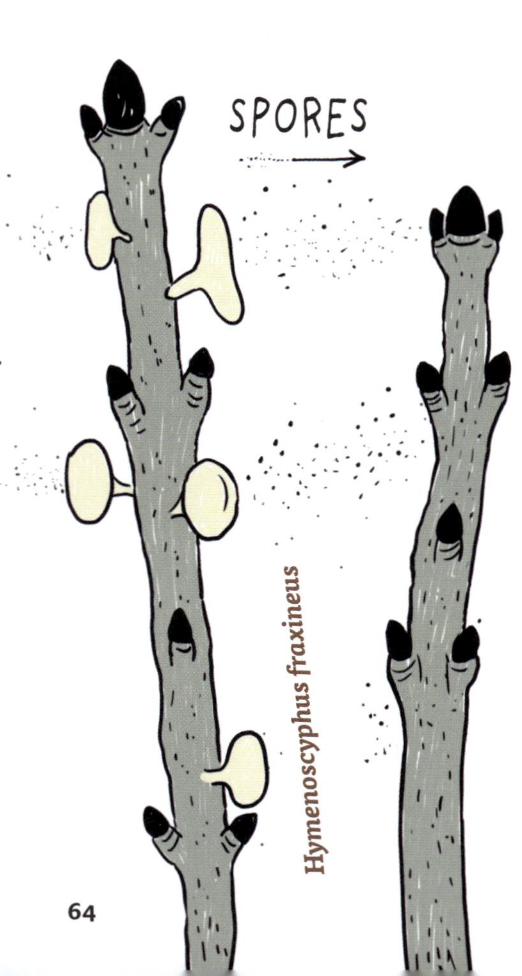


Not all wood fungi are patient. Some start gnawing at the wood while the tree is still alive. This isn't easy for them, because a tree doesn't just let it happen. First of all, it has a sturdy layer of bark to keep wood-eaters out. Second, the tree defends itself on the inside with substances that fungi don't like. Thanks to these defense systems, a fungus doesn't usually manage to grow in living wood, but sometimes it does. It may succeed if the tree is weakened by age or drought, for example, or if its roots have been damaged by a digger. If a beech is weakened, the giant polypore seizes its chance. Even healthy trees sometimes fall victim to fungus. *Hymenoscyphus fraxineus* penetrates the branches of the ash tree with its threads and causes a disease called "ash dieback." Eventually, the ash tree dies. By then, the fungus has already grown its tiny mushrooms out of the branches and its spores have blown to new ash branches.

There are also some fungi that don't wait for leaves to fall to the ground in autumn. They start growing into the leaves in the summer. Often they don't really harm the tree. Only when the leaves fall in autumn do they really start to eat and grow properly. They just like to get in on the feast early.

## Nibbling at plants

Apart from trees, fungi also like other plants and plant-like organisms. Even the smallest ones can't escape. Diatoms, for example, are a type of algae that is well defended against algae-eaters. They have armor as hard as glass, often with sharp spines. But even that doesn't protect them from water-dwelling single-celled fungi.

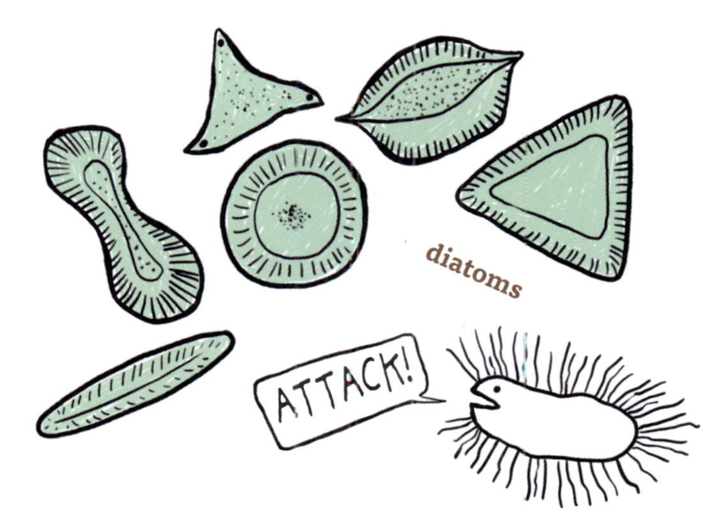

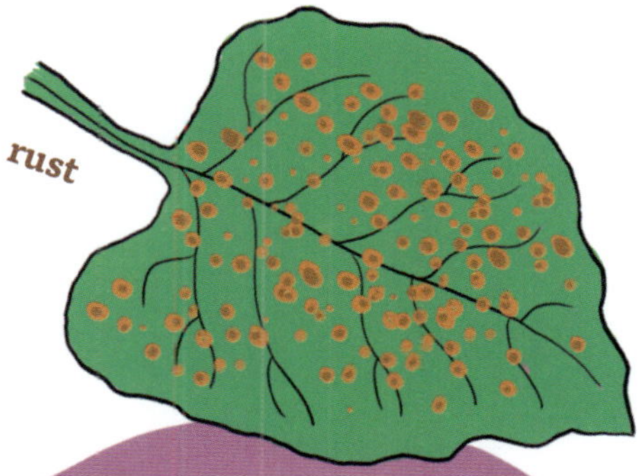

rust

**Smuts** and **rusts** have a bad name around farmers. We're not talking about rusty tractors or smutty jokes, but the fungi with those names. They eat away at crops that then turn black or brown and die. When they find a whole field of their favorite plant, smuts and rusts (also called **blights**) are unstoppable.

MILDEW!

**Mildew** is the name for fungi that often grow on living leaves. Some types of mildew make plants sick.

# Fungus eats fungus

Some fungi eat fungi. Not themselves, of course, but other species. This often happens on the sly, meaning we don't see, but the species that make mushrooms are sometimes caught out. For instance, you often see witch's butter near bark fungi. It's not just hanging out for fun. Inside the tree bark, the fungal threads of the witch's butter are eating the fungal threads of the bark fungus.

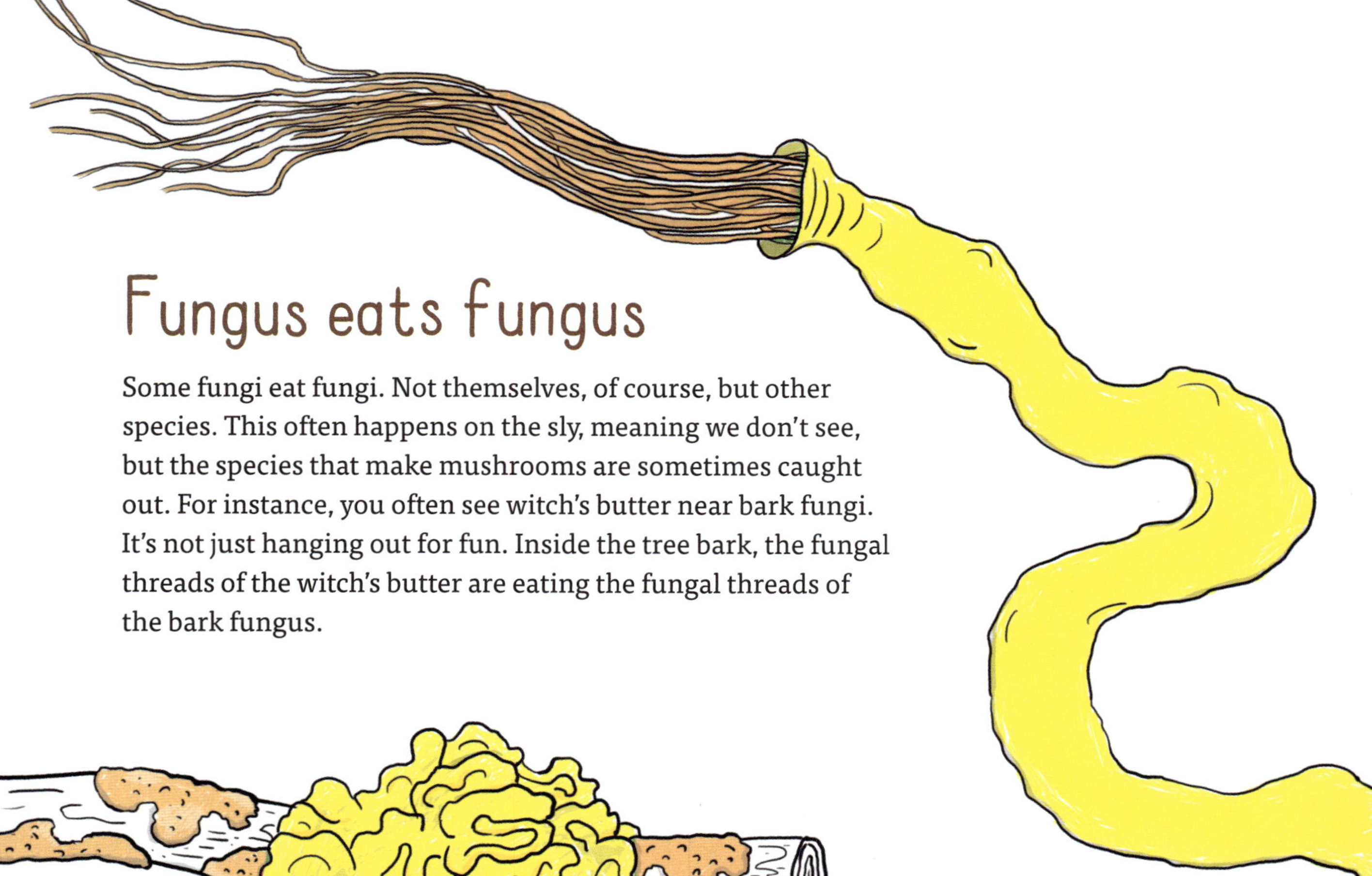


But more often than not, fungus-eaters are harmless cleaners. After the *Russula* mushroom has done its job, it is often eaten by a silky piggyback (*Asterophora*). This fungus rapidly makes its own fungal network and its own mushrooms, which grow out of the *Russula*. Mushrooms growing out of a mushroom—that's funny!

silky piggyback

*Russula*

Name: **collared earthstar** | Scientific name: ***Geastrum triplex***

Looks like a flower but really is a mushroom—a puffball, to be more precise. It shoots dark brown spores from the little hole in the ball.

# Carnivores

You know what predators are. But predatory fungi? Do they exist too? They do! There are even fungi that catch worms with a lasso. They don't hunt large earthworms, but small pale roundworms called "nematodes." There are thousands of these in the ground. Many of them live off fungi, but cup fungi turn the tables. They make little loops with their fungal filaments under the ground. If an unsuspecting worm accidentally crawls through it, the loop closes. It's actually more like the snare a hunter might use to catch a rabbit than a cowboy's lasso.

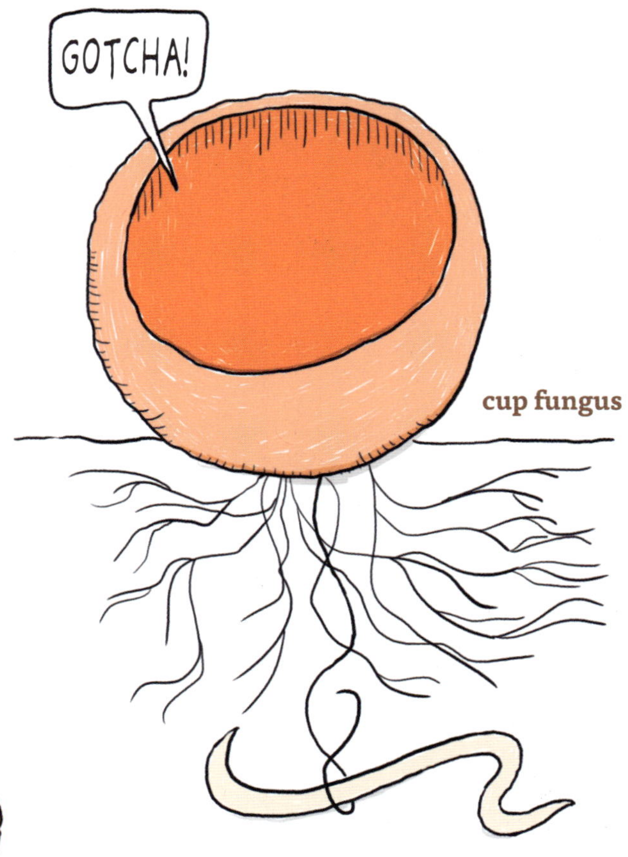


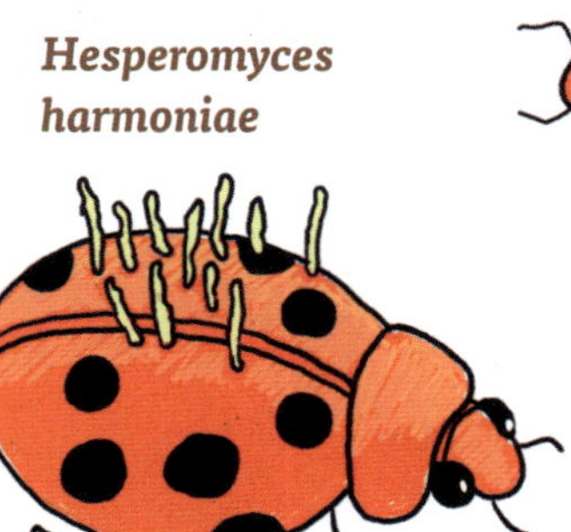


## Flies and butterflies

Flies and other insects are sometimes the victims of a fungus that hunts insects. Often, these fungi specialize in a single type of insect. Since there are many species of insect, there are also many different types of insect-eating fungus.

Some are super-specialized. These live, for example, only on the antennae of a particular beetle species, and they do so very carefully, without bothering the beetle.

Most insect-eaters are less innocent. Often, they are really sneaky. They kill their victim, but not directly. It starts with a spore landing on a fly. That spore germinates and grows a bit on the insect. Most of the food is inside the fly, so the fungus wants to get inside too. If it doesn't find a hole, the fungus makes one itself.

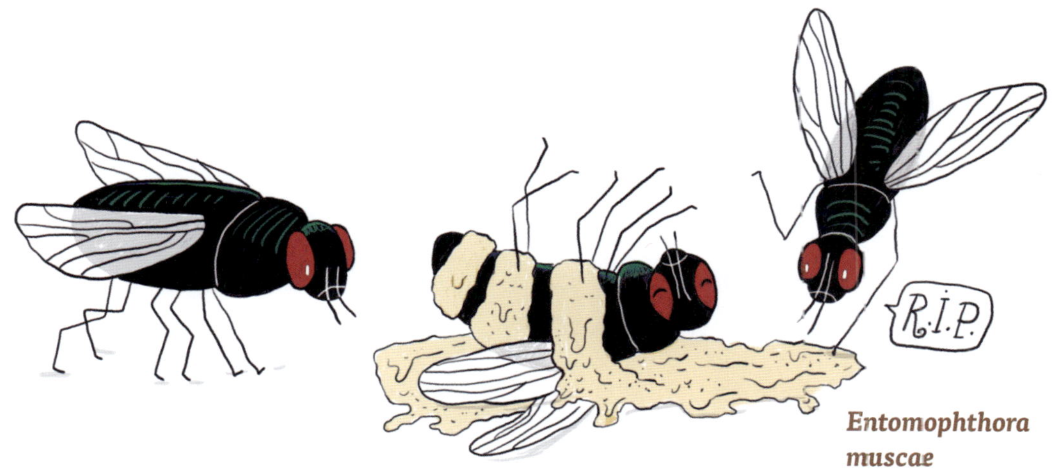

*Entomophthora muscae*

To do this, a fungal cell makes a hard little bud and squirts water into it with great force. With a pressure five times that of a bicycle tire pump, the fungus bores through the insect's hard exoskeleton and starts to eat and grow. The fly doesn't realize a thing, not even when it has already been half-eaten inside, because the clever fungus saves the most important body parts until last. Eventually, it all gets to be too much for the fly. Dazed, it lands on a windowsill and dies. Soon after that, a yellowy-white goo full of spores oozes from the fly. When a healthy fly comes to say goodbye to its dead friend, the fungus has yet another prey to catch.

Some fungi make their homes inside caterpillars. Here, too, the fungus takes its time. First it lets the caterpillar eat its fill, grow, and find a place to pupate. A safe place an inch or so underground, for example. That's when the fungus makes its move. Its fungal network eats and grows, and instead of a butterfly, a mushroom emerges from the cocoon.

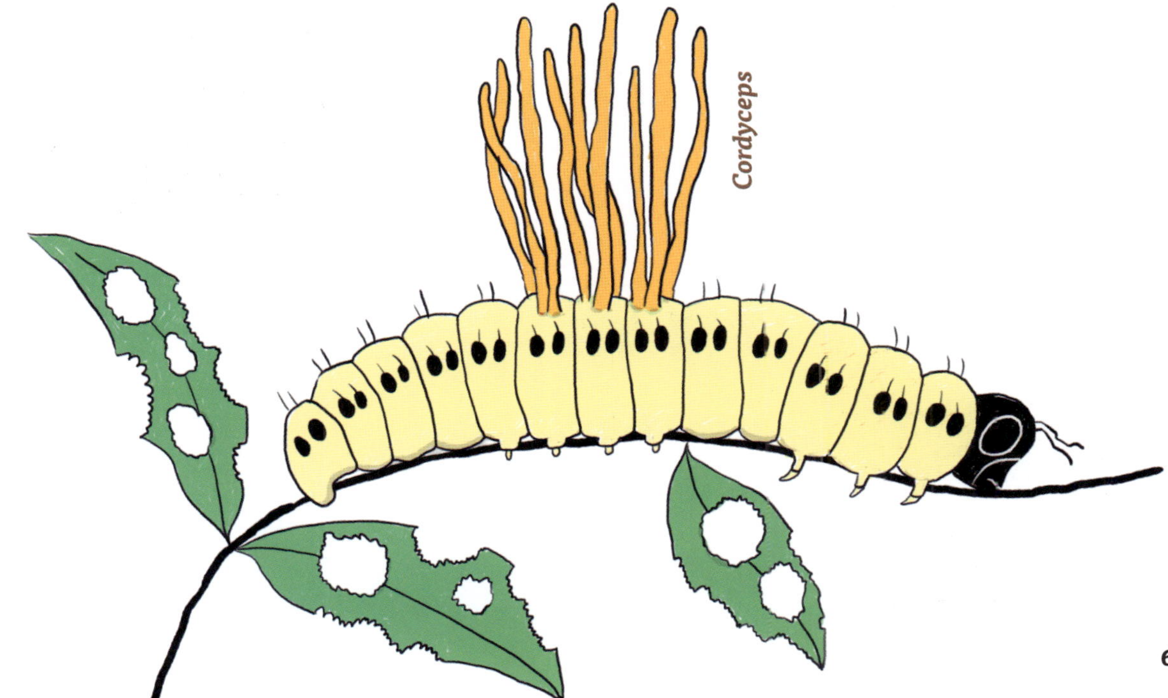
*Cordyceps*

### A six-legged zombie

*Ophiocordyceps* is a fungus found in tropical rainforests. It lives in wood ants and can control its victim's behavior—to its own benefit, of course. You can read how it does this in these two diaries.

**From the diary of a wood ant:**

**June 3**
Had a good day, worked hard.

**June 4**
Felt a bit weird today.

**June 5**
Didn't feel like working. Didn't feel like company either. I did really feel like climbing, though!

**June 6**
Had to climb up. Now I'm on the underside of a leaf, my jaws clamped around its central vein. No idea what I'm doing. Feels very strange. Well, actually, I don't feel much at all . . .

## From the diary of an *Ophiocordyceps* fungus:

**June 3**
I've grown all the way through the wood ant. Tomorrow I'll strike.

**June 4**
Started. Let's see how it goes.

**June 5**
It's working: my ant is doing what I want it to do!

**June 6**
I've sent it to a perfect spot. Mission accomplished, ant! Now it's my turn.

**June 13**
I am full, the ant is empty. My mushroom is ready to grow outside.

**July 4**
What a great mushroom! Lots of wood ants under me: time to release my spores!

Once a wood ant has been hijacked by the fungus, its loses its own will and turns into a zombie. Because of this, *Ophiocordyceps* is also called the "zombie ant fungus."

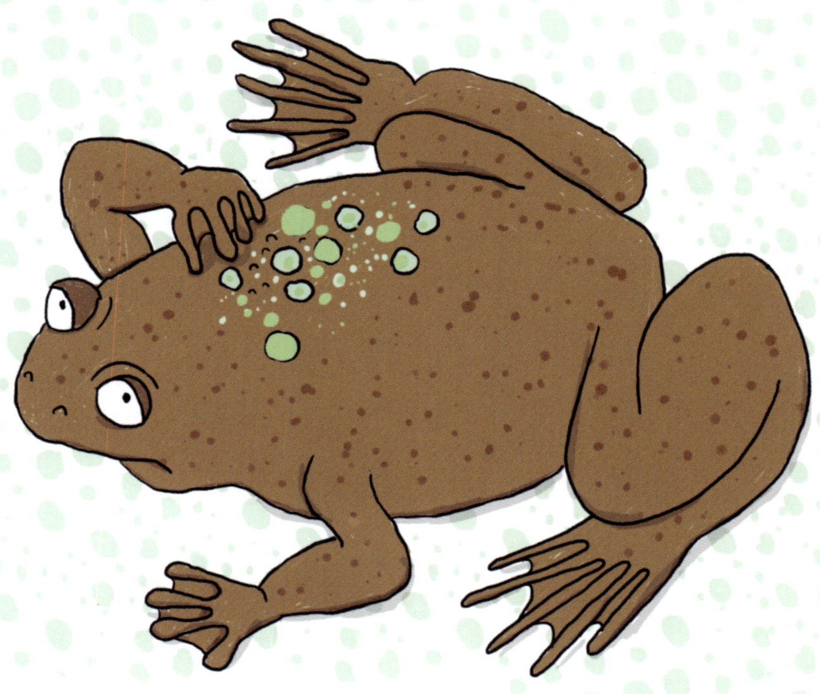

# Frog-eaters

Frogs and salamanders love wet places, and so do fungi. Some fungi love wet frog or salamander skin too. They poke little holes in it and eat some—just the outer layer, not too much. This has been going on for millions of years, and usually it works out fine. But in 1998, things started going wrong. That was when frog biologists in the rainforests of Panama noticed that a lot of frogs were disappearing. The creatures were getting sick and dying in droves. That same year, frog biologists in Australian rainforests saw the same thing. And in the years that followed, it got worse and worse—which was a shame for all those colorful rainforest frogs. Some had only just been discovered, and they died out shortly afterward. They were often poisonous frogs. Nothing wanted to eat them—except for a frog skin fungus.

**The fungus that makes frogs and salamanders sick belongs to the phylum Chytridiomycota.**

How it happened, we don't know, but probably the biologists themselves were to blame. Well, they and the African clawed frog, a favorite laboratory animal for biologists worldwide. There's an aquarium containing these animals at every university. It turns out that clawed frogs often have a skin fungus. This isn't a problem for them. They have enough resistance, so the fungus stays small. And the African frogs don't suffer much from their skin fungus; it's just a little itchy. So the frogs scratch the itch with their claws—no big deal.

What *is* a big deal is that the biologists could have carried traces of that scratched-off frog skin fungus with them from their lab to the rainforest. Accidentally, of course, on the sole of a shoe or something. For the poison frogs in Australia and Panama, it was a new fungus. A kind of frog COVID that they didn't have any resistance to, so the fungus destroyed their delicate skin.

Since then, some frogs seem to be coping a bit better, but the frog disease has not yet run its course. To make matters worse, a salamander skin fungus emerged in the Netherlands in 2010. Sick, dying, and dead fire salamanders were found in the south of the country. Fire salamanders are poisonous, just like those tropical frogs. But the fungus didn't care about that. Meanwhile, the beautiful yellow and black salamander is almost extinct there now, and it's not doing very well in neighboring Belgium either. It hasn't arrived in North America yet, but people are very concerned.

# Fungus as prey

The soil is full of fungal threads and creepy-crawlies nibbling away: mites, worms, wood lice . . . But what do they nibble away at? Dead leaves, as you probably know. But only a bit; they actually like fungal threads better. They are easier to digest than those dead leaves full of cellulose and lignin.

And ladybugs? You've probably learned that they eat aphids. That's true for the most common species, but there are some that prefer to graze on fungi. The yellow 22-spot ladybird eats only the fungus growing on living leaves.

# Taking a bite

By now you know that a mushroom consists of a lot of fungal threads, closely packed together. For mold lovers, a fungal mass is a real feast. All kinds of animals like to nibble at them. Squirrels like to take bites out of king boletes, and wood mice like to sink their teeth into mushrooms too. What's more, maggots and other insect larvae live in almost every mushroom. The insect mothers look for a young mushroom and lay their eggs in it. These hatch quickly—mushrooms aren't around for long, after all—and then the larvae eat their fill. With all those bugs inside, a meal of forest mushrooms is not as vegetarian as you might think! But as you probably know: not every mushroom simply allows itself to be eaten. Some taste nasty; others are even deadly poisonous. Wild animals seem to know exactly which ones to stay away from. Humans find it harder, even with good books to help guide them.

There are also all kinds of bacteria that eat fungi: dead fungi and sometimes live ones. But just as mushrooms can contain substances that are toxic to animals and humans, they can also make substances that are toxic to bacteria. These bacteria poisons are called **antibiotics**.

# Soil and rainwater

This chapter started with the role of fungi in nature. So far, it has mostly been about eating and being eaten, which is quite important. But that isn't the whole story. To properly appreciate the importance of fungi, imagine for a moment that you are a plant. A tree, a shrub, a clump of grass, or a daisy. What do you think is most important to you? That's right: good soil that you can stand in with your roots. With delicious **humus** (hyoo-muss) in it. No, not the chickpea puree. That's written differently (hummus) and pronounced differently too. Humus is digested plant matter, largely the work of fungi. Soil with lots of humus holds rainwater like a sponge. And where the fungal threads break down or disappear, air channels form. Airy and moist, there's no finer soil for a plant.

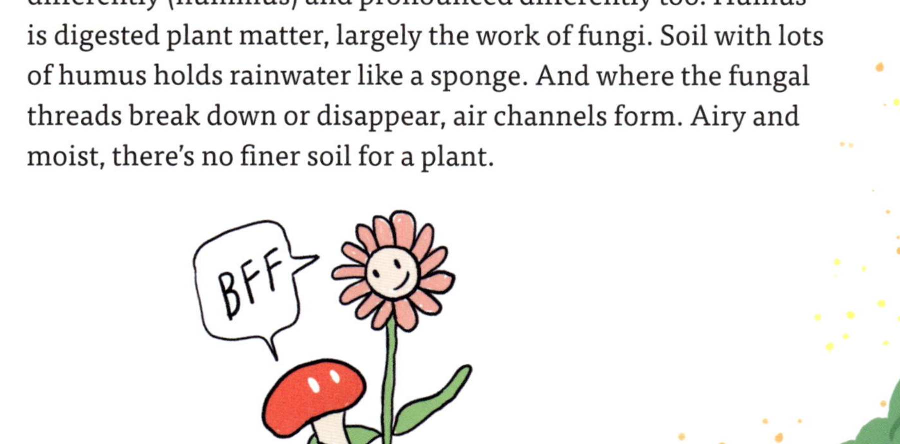


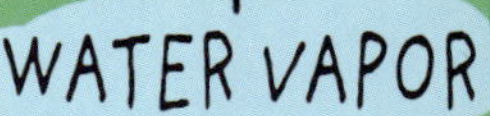


One teaspoon of good forest soil can contain over a mile (2 kilometers) of fungal threads.

# Rainmakers

Tasty soil. What more would you want as a plant? A nice shower, of course. And what do fungi have to do with that? More than you'd think. To understand this, you need to know how rain is made.

It starts with water vapor. There's a lot of this in the warm, humid air close to the ground. Then, as the air rises, it cools. Because the higher you get, the colder it gets. The water vapor wants to become water again. But this only works if the vapor can find something to cling onto up there. A particle of dust is all right, but a fungal spore is a real magnet for water droplets. And there's a huge number of spores floating in the air, particularly above rainforests. A lot of fungi grow there, and so a lot of spores are blown into the air. It's possible that it rains a lot in rainforests *because* of these fungal spores. Better there than over the sea, where nobody benefits. The rainforest itself is delighted with these downpours: that's why it's called a rainforest, and why it's so green.

So fungi are very useful in nature. Okay, they can be a nuisance at times, but they always clean up their own messes, and others' too. All in all, by eating, growing, and releasing spores, they make nature a nice place to live. Plants are especially happy to have fungi around. After all, beautiful friendships arise between good neighbors. Friends for life.

**Tons of spores**
**There are 55 million tons (50 billion kilograms) of spores floating in the air around Earth at any given time: enough to give every human 13 pounds (6 kilograms)!**

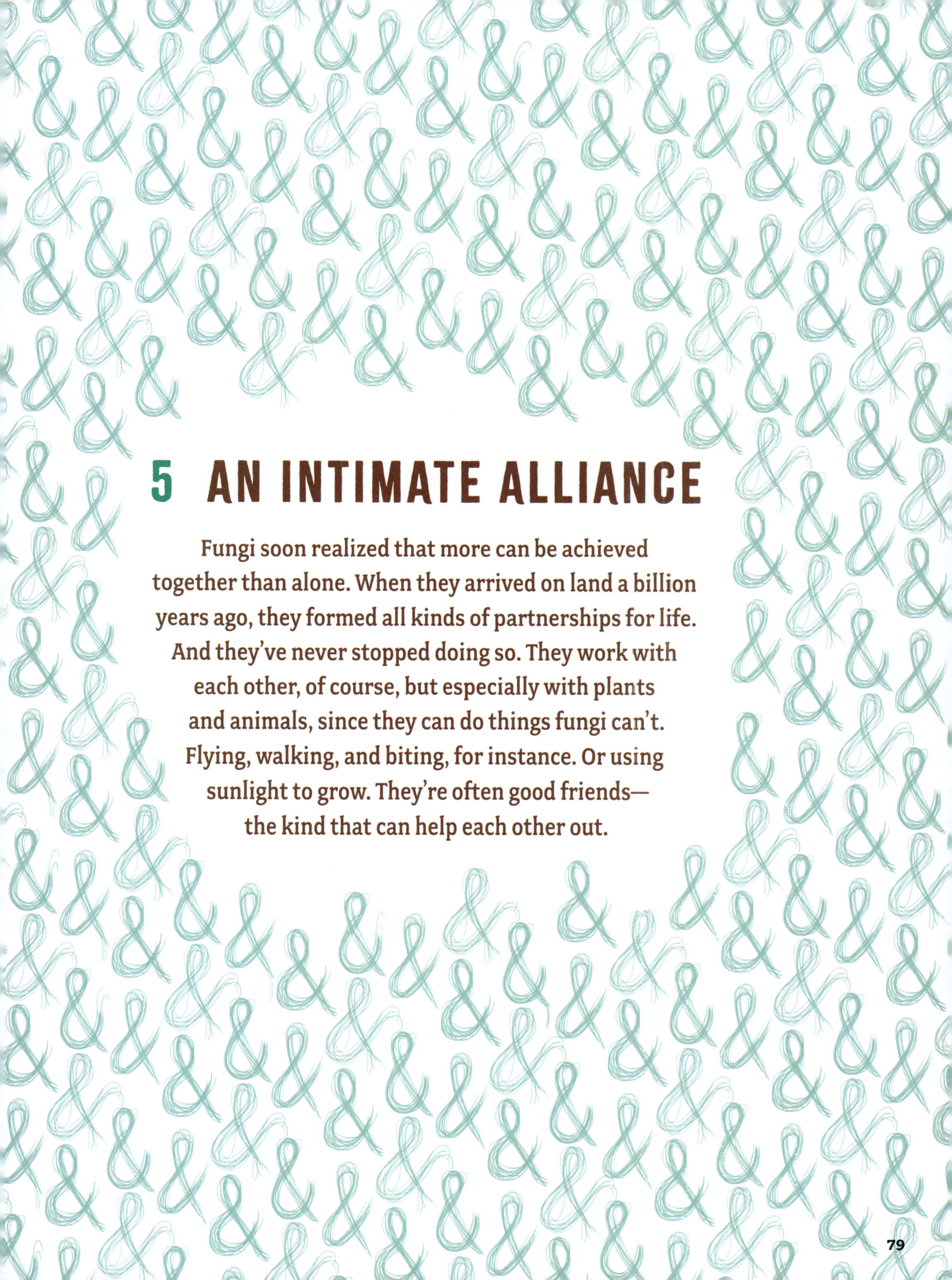

# 5 AN INTIMATE ALLIANCE

Fungi soon realized that more can be achieved together than alone. When they arrived on land a billion years ago, they formed all kinds of partnerships for life. And they've never stopped doing so. They work with each other, of course, but especially with plants and animals, since they can do things fungi can't. Flying, walking, and biting, for instance. Or using sunlight to grow. They're often good friends—the kind that can help each other out.

# Living with plants

Not many people know that fungi live in *all* plants. Yes, in the previous chapter, you learned that fungi grow on and in some plants, and that plants can get sick from them. But most fungi don't harm their plant host. Fungi always grow on the bark and branches of trees. *Just let them get on with their lives*, the trees probably think.

## Leaf-dwellers

Even when fungi grow on their leaves, the trees aren't usually affected very much. In tropical rainforests, there are many species of fungi that can live only on leaves. They *live on* them; they don't eat them. The leaf molds catch their food from the air. Pollen grains, wood dust, that kind of thing. The fungi are modest: they grow mainly on the underside of leaves, because they don't want to block out light. They are tidy guests, those leaf fungi, but they don't really do much to help the trees.

When two or more different species live together, it's called **symbiosis** (sim-by-oh-sis).

The network of fungal threads fused with plant roots is called a **mycorrhiza** (my-cor-ry-za). Many species of forest mushrooms form mycorrhizae with trees.

## Too thick, too short

It's different with the fungi in the soil. You already know they make good soil—soil with humus, nice and airy and moist. But they do a lot more for the trees, and for just about all plants, in fact. Soil fungi slurp up water for their green friends. The water contains dissolved substances that are at least as important to the plants as the water itself. Can't the plants drink it themselves, you might ask, with their roots? If you put a plant with its roots in a vase with water, the roots will drink the water. But in the ground things are different. To get to water, the tree roots need to wriggle between all the grains of sand and humus particles, and they are too thick for that. Only the thinnest roots can manage, but they are much too short. Fortunately, the roots get help from their underground fungus friends. Their fungal threads grow far into the soil from the roots.

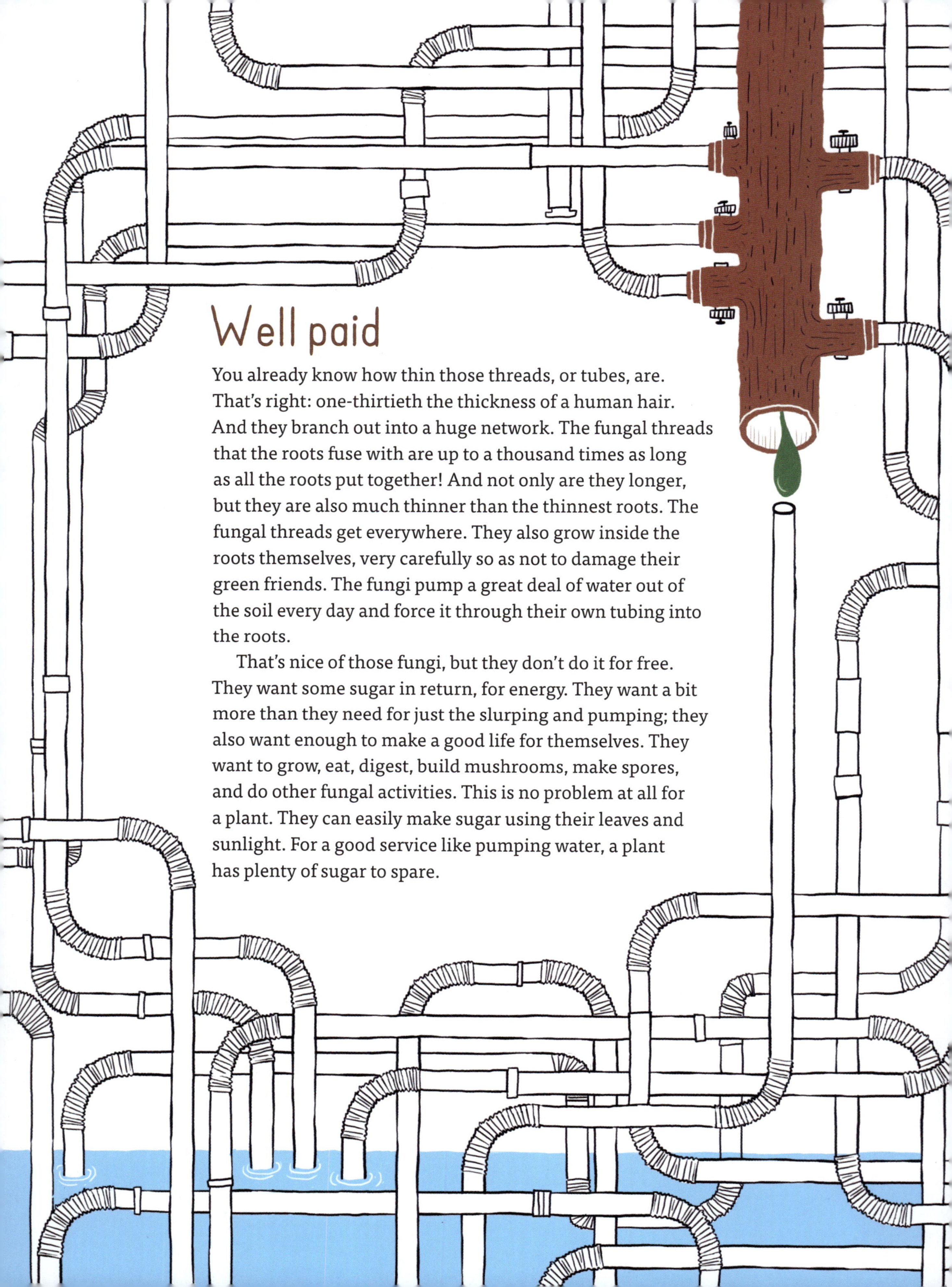

# Well paid

You already know how thin those threads, or tubes, are. That's right: one-thirtieth the thickness of a human hair. And they branch out into a huge network. The fungal threads that the roots fuse with are up to a thousand times as long as all the roots put together! And not only are they longer, but they are also much thinner than the thinnest roots. The fungal threads get everywhere. They also grow inside the roots themselves, very carefully so as not to damage their green friends. The fungi pump a great deal of water out of the soil every day and force it through their own tubing into the roots.

That's nice of those fungi, but they don't do it for free. They want some sugar in return, for energy. They want a bit more than they need for just the slurping and pumping; they also want enough to make a good life for themselves. They want to grow, eat, digest, build mushrooms, make spores, and do other fungal activities. This is no problem at all for a plant. They can easily make sugar using their leaves and sunlight. For a good service like pumping water, a plant has plenty of sugar to spare.

# Everybody's friend

Soil fungi are often not very picky about their friendships. Some do have a preference, though. For instance, the fungal threads of the fly agaric and the roots of birch trees really like each other. You can often spot the red-and-white-dotted mushrooms near the trees with the white trunks. But the fly agaric also likes to make friends with oaks and beeches. Or with pines and spruces, quite different sorts of tree. Most soil fungi are friends with everyone. And it's not that a tree only has one fungus friend. Under the ground, a large tree will be fused with more than 50 fungi of sometimes 15 different species.

The underground cooperation between plants and fungi is not a recent thing. It has existed since plants first emerged from the sea onto land. The first plants didn't even have roots, so they were totally dependent on their fungal friends for underground work.

# Networking, fungal style

Under the ground, plants are attached to multiple fungi, and fungi to multiple plants. This means that plants are also connected to each other via the fungal web. We've known for a while that trees, in particular, probably communicate with each other through this web. Yes, you read that right: some scientists think that trees exchange information on the fungal web. They explain where to get the best nutrients, warn each other when nasty leaf-nibblers are hanging around, and exchange other interesting tree talk.

Information travels from one tree to another via a fungal tube, and so does sugary water. The trees appear to be helping each other. An old oak helps a sapling, and spruces help birches through a difficult winter. It sounds wonderful, and maybe even too good to be true. The reality is perhaps slightly different. The fungi are probably in charge. They move sugared water around because they want to keep both spruce and birch trees alive. If a birch is weakened, the fungus borrows some sugar from the spruce and pumps it toward the birch. In spring, the birch grows fresh leaves and makes enough sugar. If the spruce struggles in summer, due to drought or another challenge, the fungus will pump the birch sugar the other way again. Does the fungus actually communicate this plan? Probably not. But it does help itself in this way, and it ends up helping the whole forest at the same time.

**All the mycorrhizal networks in a forest are sometimes called the wood wide web. This is a pun on World Wide Web—the information system we know as the internet, and the spelled-out form of the "www" you often see in front of a website address.**

Name: **shaggy mane** or **shaggy inkcap** | Scientific name: ***Coprinus comatus***
Often found in grass, and sometimes on the street. Can break through asphalt. There's never just one, always several, and together they can look like a herd of sheep in the grass. Until they turn black and start dripping . . .

# Feeding babies

It's not easy for baby plants. The seeds they germinate from don't contain much food. There's just enough to make the first stalk, leaves, and root. That little root has to quickly search for fungi, so the plant baby cries out for help. Not with sound, of course, but with a special substance. If a soil fungus senses it, it grows toward the baby plant.

That special substance can cause something else to happen as well: it can prompt fungal spores to germinate. Spores can lie in wait in the ground for years waiting for a signal. When they smell the substance from the plant's seed, the spores burst open. The fungal thread grows toward the young plant and they become friends for life.

Orchids have tiny seeds. This is handy, because they can be easily blown by the wind to a new spot. And if the seeds are very small, the mother plant can make lots of them without much effort. The problem is that not all fungi can live with orchids. And a bigger problem is that the tiny orchid seed has absolutely no ability to feed itself. It can't even make its own first root. That's why orchids give each seed a tiny piece of the right kind of fungus. If the seed ends up somewhere suitable, the fungus starts growing. Only when the fungus can absorb enough water does it wake up its orchid seed. Without its fungus, an orchid seed can't germinate.

**Ghost plants**

**Some orchid species get a bit carried away with their underground fungus. Actually, make that *a lot* carried away. The lazy orchids refuse to make chlorophyll. If a plant can't make food from sunlight and air, it's not really a plant anymore. All of the lazy orchid's food comes from its fungal friend. Whether the friend is happy with the orchid, we don't know, but it can live with it. The plant kingdom has other cheaters too. They are easy to pick out. Just look for plants without leaves and with pale stems that are light brown, or sometimes even white. Only their flowers may have color.**

# An ancient alliance

Perhaps the most weird and wonderful collaboration between fungi and plants, and the closest and most successful, is **lichen** (lie-ken). A lichen might look like a curious little plant, but it's actually a fungus containing tiny algae. The fungus provides the shape, it grips to a safe place, and it can drink. And the algae provide the food. Like plants, they do so with sunlight and air. These lichen partners have been getting by for hundreds of millions of years like this.

Lichens probably grew on land earlier than plants. The fungi and algae in lichen form make a good team because they don't even need soil. The fungus can cling onto bare rock and extract water directly from the air. It simply draws the water vapor to itself. The only drawback is that lichen grows slowly, sometimes only tenths of an inch (a few millimeters) a year. But they have time. A lichen never gets very big, but it can grow where plants can't survive. Lichen live in tricky habitats, from the North and South Poles to high mountains, from tree trunks to roof tiles.

The fungus part of the lichen can make spores. If those spores germinate, they need to be lucky enough to have some algae nearby. And it has to be the right kind, because the fungus doesn't want to live with just any old alga. This is why lichens prefer to spread as a clump of fungus with some algae already in it.

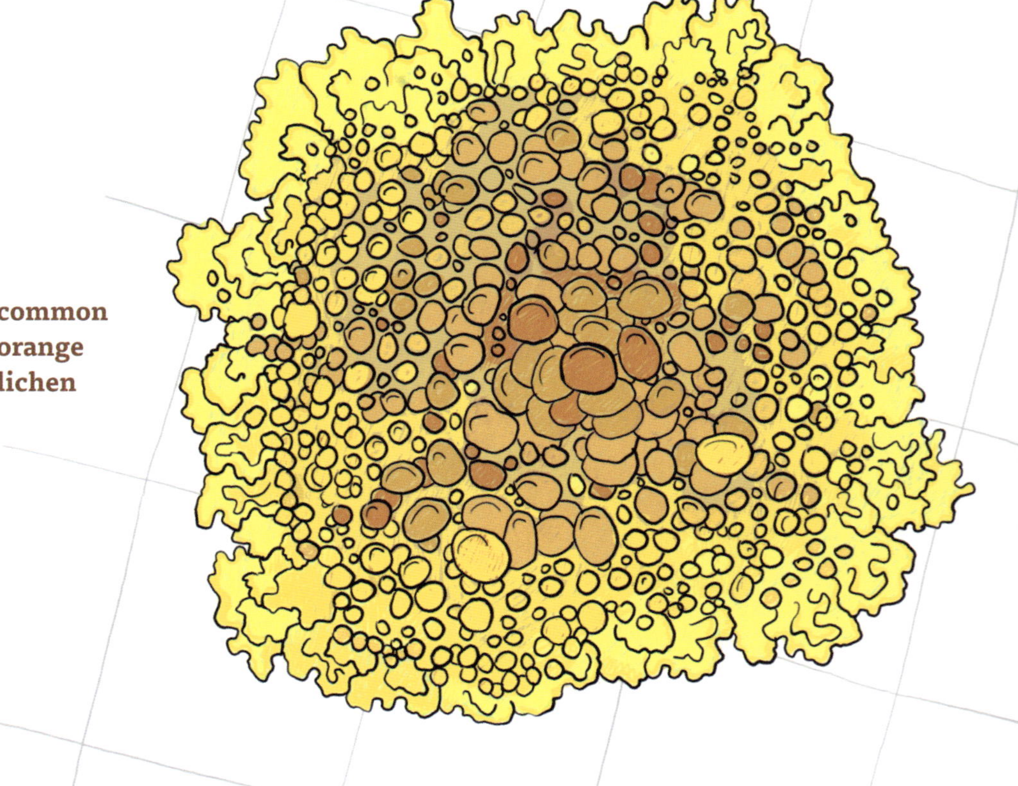

**common orange lichen**

**Life in a lichen commune**
A lichen consists of a fungus and an alga. In other words, two different species. At least, that's what was thought until recently. But we have learned that many more species live in the fungus: a whole army of different bacteria. And apart from the main fungus, there are a whole bunch of other fungi too. They probably have a job to do, and they certainly feel at home there, nice and protected. A lichen is one cozy commune!

Name: **madame's pixie cup** | Scientific name: ***Cladonia coccifera***

A lichen fit for a tea party. This lichen—a fungus that grows together with algae—can even survive in dry sand. Spores are made inside its bright red tips.

# Living with animals

If you go to a rainforest in South America, you'll definitely see some animals. No, we don't mean jaguars and tapirs. They do live there, but they're shy and rare. You can spot macaws, toucans, and hummingbirds, but they are often high in the treetops. The first animals you're likely to see in the jungle are ants. Chances are they'll be walking around waving a chunk of leaf above their heads. A piece of leaf they've chewed off. These are leaf-cutter ants.

## Leaf soup

The ants march up tall trees in long rows and come back down again with a bit of green leaf between their jaws. They carry these snippets to their underground nest, where they live with several million of their own kind. The bits of leaves are not for themselves, but for the fungi that the leaf-cutter ants live with. Or, depending on how you want to describe it, for the mushrooms that the ants are farming. The ants take the pieces of leaves to the hundreds of cellar rooms they've dug, each the size of a football. The ants can't do anything with the leaves themselves; they are indigestible. But their housemates, the fungi, can digest them—especially in the nice, warm, humid rooms the ants have built for their fungal friends. And especially if the ants first chew them up into a green goo. The fungus digests the leaf pulp and then eats it. It grows well, and soon it produces white balls at the tips of its fungal threads. These are for the ants, as a thank-you. The leaf-cutter ants are happy: the fungal balls make perfect ant food. They live off them and feed them to the ant larvae in their underground nurseries. All that climbing and cutting, lugging and chewing, feeding and building is hard work, but it's worth it: leaf-cutter ants are the most successful animals in the rainforest.

FUNGUS

# Wood pudding

Termites are insects that look like ants, but they aren't actually related. Unlike ants, you only find them in hot countries, but like ants, many thousands live together in a self-built nest. The termite mounds in Africa are particularly impressive. Some are up to 26 feet (8 meters) high. On the inside, their palace is even more impressive. This mound is not only the termites' home, but also a mushroom farm. A lot of it is specially built for the fungus the termites live with. The nest contains special growing chambers where the termites feed their fungal friend goop made from pre-chewed wood and other tough plant stuff. And their own poo! Inside the nest is a complete air-conditioning system, with a basement to the water table and cooling plates on the ceiling, double walls, and ventilation pipes that can stretch 3 feet (1 meter) high.

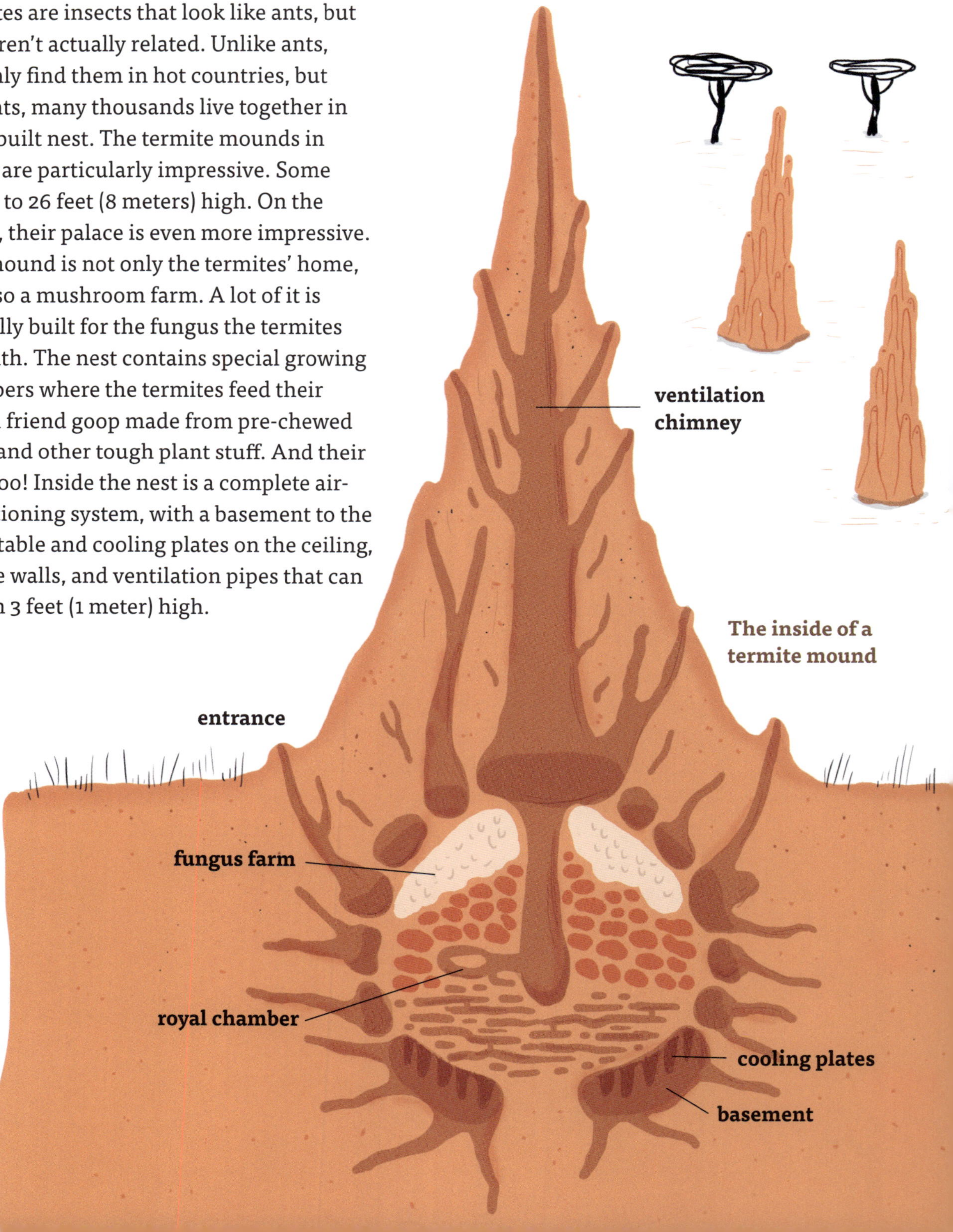

**ventilation chimney**

**The inside of a termite mound**

**entrance**

**fungus farm**

**royal chamber**

**cooling plates**

**basement**

Name: **coral jelly fungus** | Scientific name: ***Calocera viscosa***
This mushroom isn't big, but it does stand out. Its flaming stalks grow from the wood of conifers. Sometimes it looks like a log is on fire.

# Belly-dwellers

Cows, horses, and sheep. Wildebeests, zebras, and bison. These are all grazers, and grazers eat grass. Grass is tough. The cell walls of grass cells are made of cellulose, which doesn't break down inside an average animal's stomach. But there are single-celled fungi that are very good at it, so grazers like to make use of them. Many grazers have several stomachs, and the first stomach is particularly large. This one is especially for fungi. It's not a stomach with burning acid like we have, but a lovely warm bath. A fungal paradise. The fungi, and some bacteria, eat away at the cell walls of the grass. Only when these are mostly digested does the grazer pass the nutritious mush on to the next stomach and then to the intestines. Quite a few fungi are swept along with the grassy mush and don't survive. But they've had a fantastic life by then, and they leave behind plenty of fungal offspring.

**Most fungi that live in the stomachs of grazers belong to the Chytridiomycota phylum (see page 51).**

# Beetle babies

Wood beetles have single-celled fungi in their stomachs and intestines. This allows them to digest wood. But most beetles don't eat much when they are adults. As children, however, they are greedy gobblers. Wood beetle larvae don't have much else to do, because they live in their food: they gnaw tunnels through the wood. So finding food isn't a problem; digesting the wood is. How does a beetle baby get the right fungus inside its belly? Its mother takes care of that. When she lays her eggs in the wood, she smears them with a bit of fungus. When a larva hatches, it starts by eating its eggshell, and eats the fungus along with it.

There are also beetle mothers who plant fungus around their newly laid eggs on the wood. The fungus starts eating the wood there and growing through it. By the time the wood beetle larva hatches, the fungus has already done the hardest work. The pre-digested wood makes healthy baby food.

By now, it should be clear that plants and animals need fungi. Some are even entwined. Not surprisingly, humans often have to deal with fungi too. And no, they aren't always our friends. Still, we can and should be glad they exist.

# 6 FUNGI AND PEOPLE

Most people don't think about fungi very much. But fungi do get into our stuff and sometimes even our bodies. Usually you won't notice them, but they can be a nuisance. In fact, some are real troublemakers. But most fungi are useful. Some people find mushrooms incredibly interesting and are real fans. It's what they do with them that is not always safe.

# Diseases and toxins

Fungi will eat all kinds of things: sandwiches, logs, books. And human flesh. They can make us sick sometimes too, not just by nibbling at us but also with their poop and pee. Or their toxins. There are about 400 fungi that can make a person sick. This is only a very small fraction of the 150,000 fungal species we know, but one is enough to cause a lot of trouble.

Fortunately, fungi rarely penetrate deep into your body. It's too hot for them in there. For our bodies, 98 degrees Fahrenheit (37 degrees Celsius) is the perfect temperature. For almost all fungi, it's deadly hot—which is a good thing. Another comforting fact is that a healthy body is perfectly capable of defending itself against anything that invades it and doesn't belong. A smart fungus knows this and prefers to stay outside.

A less comforting fact is that pills, potions, and ointments are better at killing troublesome bacteria than troublesome fungi. This is not such good news, especially when we're talking about a serious fungal disease.

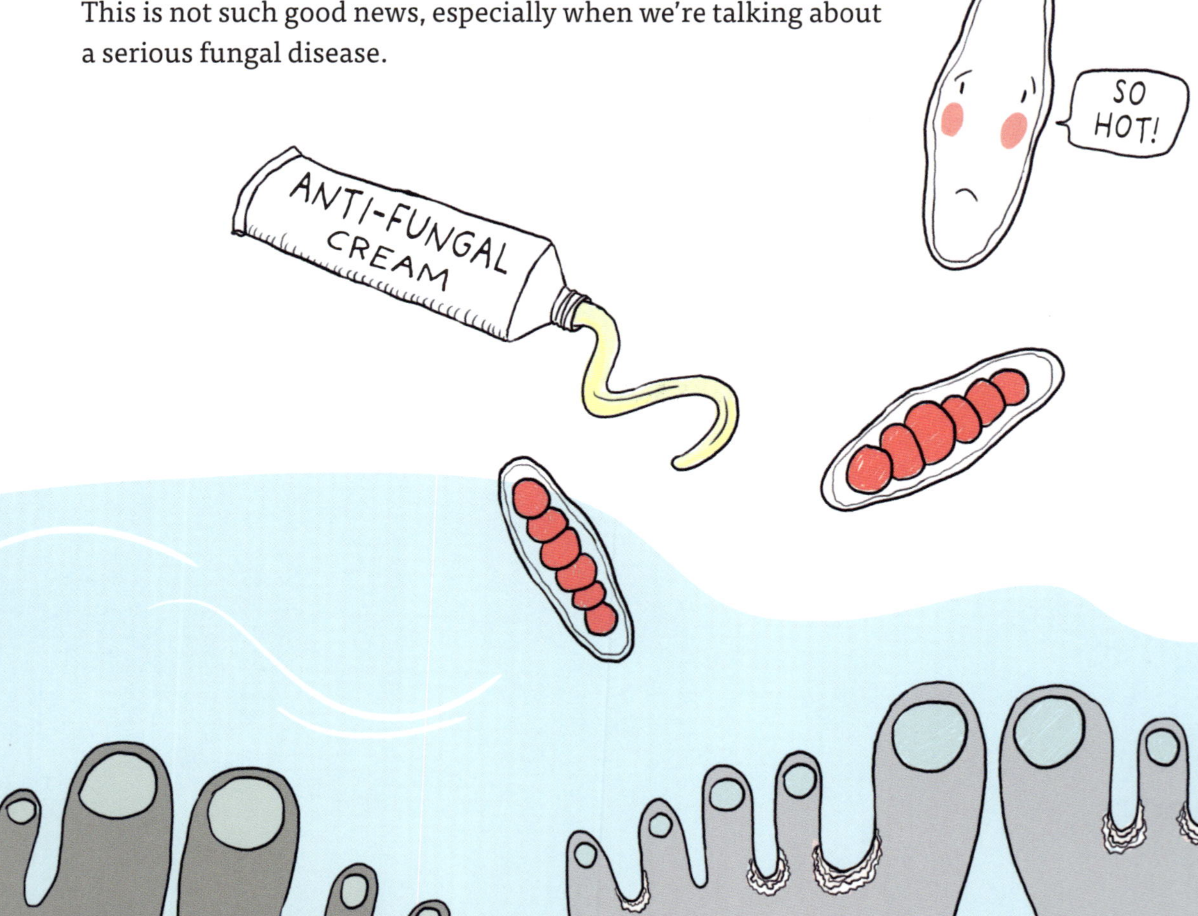

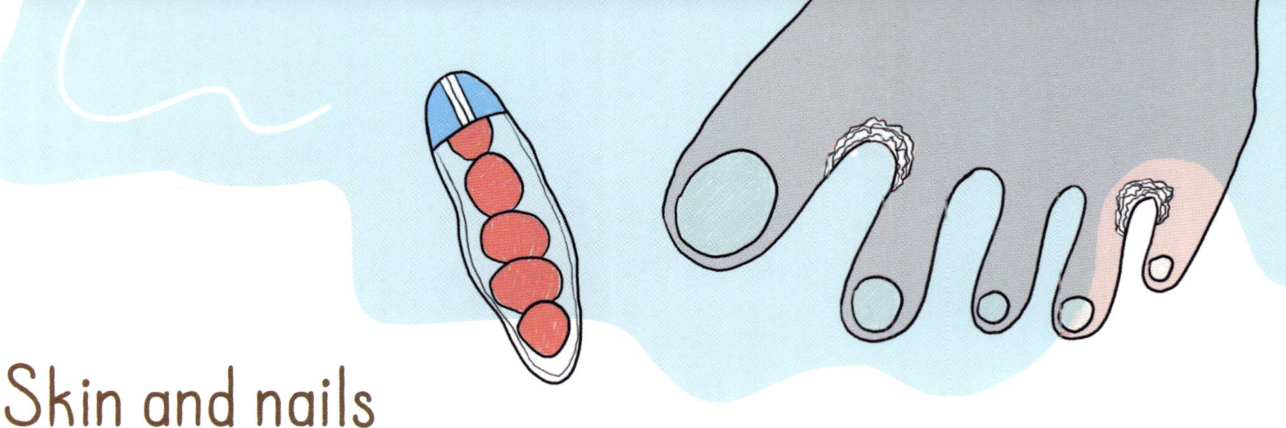

# Skin and nails

Most fungi don't get beyond our nails and the outer layer of our skin. Our skin and nails are what they come across first, and there's no blood flowing through nails and the top layer of the skin. Human blood is full of defense cells, which immediately attack invaders. A toenail or a callus (a hard bit of skin on your foot) is a lot safer for a fungus. Not many fungi can digest calluses or nails and then eat them, but there are some that can. They are the cousins of the fungi that clean up the hair and hooves of dead animals in nature.

Skin fungi are particularly happy in between our toes. Often you don't notice much, a little itching perhaps. But when your skin starts splitting, it can get sore. Some foot fungi spread easily to other feet. This can happen on the wet shower floor at a gym or swimming pool, which is where the name **athlete's foot** comes from. A special cream will get rid of it.

Foot fungus can also bore into toenails. They like the big toenail the most. And once they're in there, it's hard to get rid of them. It's not very nice, a crumbly yellow toenail, but it's not a big deal either. And it's not something you need to worry about, because children's nails don't go moldy that easily.

**Good skin fungi**

**Along with bacteria and tiny mites, thousands of single-celled fungi live on every piece of human skin. These yeasts do no harm. They eat some skin flakes, oil, and bacteria, and don't leave much mess behind.**

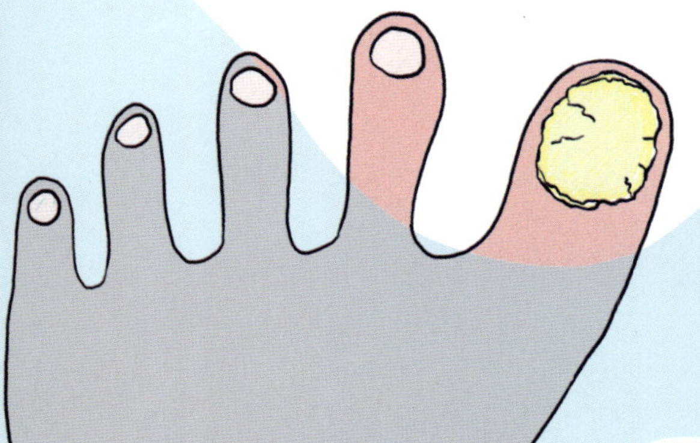

# Ruthless killers

There are some serious fungal diseases, though. Some fungi, for example, can go berserk in the lungs. This is a serious issue worldwide: more than a million people every year die of aspergillosis. But as bad as it is for the people it happens to, if you are young and healthy, and you live in a rich Western country, using a cellphone while riding your bicycle is a bigger risk than a fungus in your lungs.

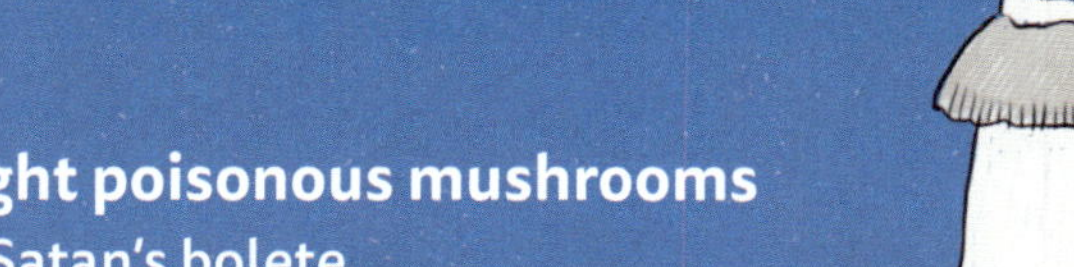

**Eight poisonous mushrooms**

1 Satan's bolete
2 false morel
3 fly agaric
4 panther cap
5 death cap
6 yellow-stainer
7 deadly fibercap
8 earthball

# Poisonous mushrooms

A poisonous mushroom doesn't attack you, but it can kill you if it accidentally ends up on your plate. Every year more than a hundred people in North America get sick from them. A handful don't survive their error. But you don't have to worry about getting poisoned if you go searching for fungi in the forest, as long as you don't eat them. You can touch even the most poisonous mushroom, the death cap, without risk. Remember to wash your hands afterward, though!

FANCY A BITE?

# Deadly bread

Some poisonous fungi get eaten by accident because they grow on something edible. In the past, one particular type of fungus caused death and destruction. It is called "ergot." This is a mold that grows on cereal grains when the plants are still growing in the field. Ergot grows mainly on rye and makes an unhealthy substance: a nerve toxin. Just a little bit makes you itch terribly, a little more makes you behave oddly, and a little more makes the blood vessels in your arms and legs go haywire and stop working. Eventually, the poison is lethal.

In the Middle Ages, many people ate rye bread. Back then, everyone had heard of the illness, and many thousands of people died from it. People still believed in witchcraft, but fortunately, in 1676, someone discovered the illness came from mold, not witches. After that, farmers, millers, and bakers started being very careful. But things still went wrong quite often. The last time that happened in Europe was in 1951, when ergot killed seven people in France. Nowadays, poisoning by this fungus almost never happens. You can eat rye bread without worrying about it.

rye with ergot

Name: **basket stinkhorn** | Scientific name: ***Clathrus ruber***
Strange basket-like ball, red or pink, the size of a tennis ball. Occurs naturally in Europe, but has been introduced in a number of places in North America. Most commonly seen (and smelled) in hot countries.

# Helping or harming?

Fungi that make plants sick can be quite a nuisance to farmers. A field contains lots of plants of the same species, set close together. If a fungus strikes one plant, soon the whole field gets sick.

In the past, farmers couldn't do anything about it. The Irish know all about this. Between 1845 and 1850, potato blight struck there. It was caused by the water mold *Phytophthora*. This is one of those fake fungi we mentioned back on page 56, but it can be a serious problem. In Ireland, 90 percent of the potato crop was lost. Since potatoes were the main food, a huge famine followed. More than a million people died, and even more fled Ireland, mostly to America. Their descendants still live there. They have plenty of potatoes to eat now, but they all know the story.

**Irish refugees**

**Without potato blight, animated film producer Walt Disney, former presidents John F. Kennedy and Joe Biden, musician Bruce Springsteen, and mobster "Whitey" Bulger would have been Irish, not American.**

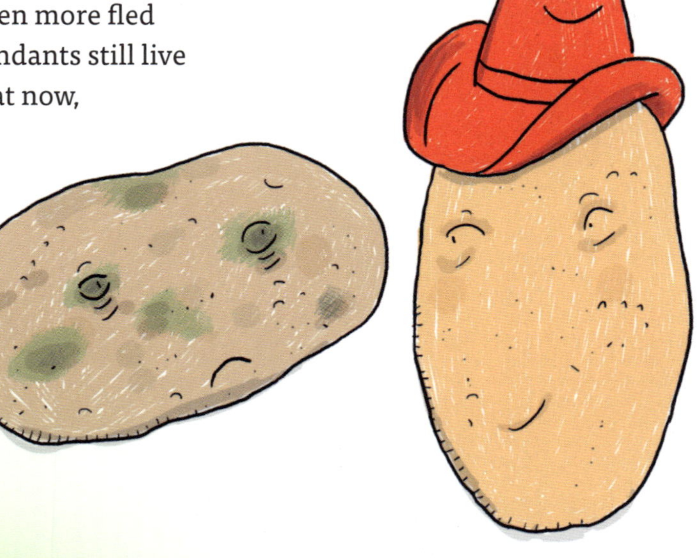

Today, there are still fungi that make agricultural crops sick. But farmers have many fungicides to spray over their fields. The fungi adapt after a while, and so do the companies making the chemicals. They invent new fungicides all the time. Farmers have less damage, but high costs. And the fungicides are not good for the soil either, or our health.

# Food-poisoners

After food has been harvested, molds often make it go bad. Food that has not been properly preserved is more likely to be eaten by fungi than by us. Instead of eating it all nicely, they eat it and then poop on it so it becomes inedible. As a result, an estimated 10 percent of everything farmers grow is lost worldwide. In other words: molds ruin as much food as 800 million people could eat. Fortunately, toxic fungi in food are well controlled.

### Three unwanted dining companions

The fungus *Magnaporthe grisea* loves rice. On its own, this species consumes as much rice as 60 million people do annually.

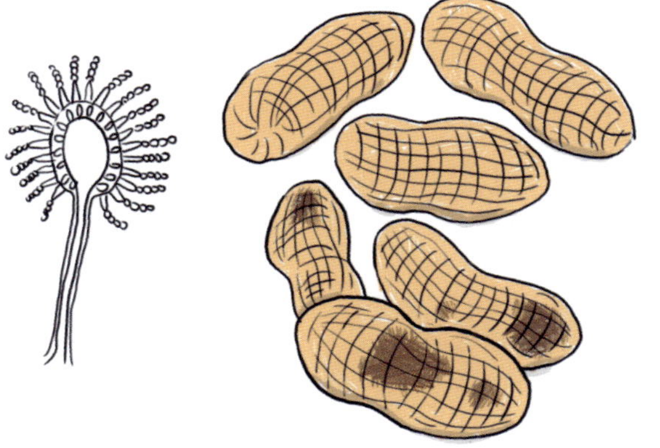

The fungus *Aspergillus flavus* loves peanuts. Not the roasted salty ones from a bag, but fresh ones from a warehouse. It's not so bad that it eats them, but the substance it makes in the process, aflatoxin, can give you cancer.

*Penicillium digitatum* turns millions of lemons and oranges into blue-green dusty balls every year. The mold might look interesting, but it makes the fruit inedible.

# Tree-fellers

Most tree fungi live peacefully with their trees, but there are some that can fell these giants. The fungus does this by growing into the tubes the tree uses to transport its water and other juices. The tree starts fighting the fungus. It usually wins, but not always. If the fungus is from a different continent, and the tree doesn't yet know how to neutralize it, it stands less of a chance.

For trees in cities, foreign tree fungi can be disastrous. Take the elm, for example. Over a century ago, elms in the Netherlands and France started getting ill, followed about 20 years later by elms in North America. The culprit was a fungus from eastern Asia. It is clearly happy in its new homes. In the last century, hundreds of thousands of trees have been killed by this fungus. Once the elm is sick, all you can do is cut it down. And quickly; otherwise, the other elms will also get Dutch elm disease.

# Beams, books, and bathrooms

Fungi can cause a lot of damage in the home. The fungus that causes "dry rot" (*Serpula lacrymans*) will eat a solid floor joist to a pulp in just a couple of years. It is said that in London during World War II this fungus destroyed more houses than bombs did. A bomb often set just one house on fire, but the water used to put it out helped dry rot on its way (the fungus gets a boost from a splash of water, and then can continue to grow without it). Neighboring houses rotted away within a year. In the dry houses of today, the fungus has much less chance to grow. But if it does, a new floor is often the only way to get rid of it.

The fungus *Stachybotrys chartarum* grows in some houses; it's often called "black mold." It may have a scary-sounding name, but it doesn't look very impressive. In damp places, however, it makes babies at lightning speed, and soon there are thousands of them—making it look like someone has sprayed black paint all around. Black mold grows especially well in musty corners. You often find it on the rubber gasket of the washing machine or on the fridge door. For most people, black mold is just ugly, but for people with asthma it is genuinely irritating. Mold cells in the air make it harder for them to breathe.

Mold can also ruin stuff. If you leave wet laundry balled up for a few days, it can develop mold spots. You can't get the stains out, and the musty smell is there to stay. Storing books in a basement or cellar often goes wrong too. Not because of bookworms, but because of mold.

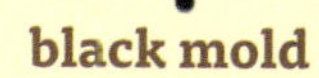

black mold

**Sick buildings**

**You sometimes hear of a building in which a suspicious number of people feel a bit unwell. They are not very sick, but still... Black mold often turns out to be the culprit. Especially if it has taken up residence in the ventilation grates.**

*Serpula lacrymans*

# Wood-improvers

It may sound odd, but wood fungus can also make wood more valuable.

• The beefsteak fungus grows on oaks and its fungal threads grow into the wood. As a result, red, flame-like stains appear in it. A cabinet made of "English brown oak" is beautiful, and a lot more expensive than a cabinet made of ordinary oak.

• Agarwood from Southeast Asia is very expensive. Not because of the wood itself, but the dark sticky sap dripping from it. This resin has a scent unlike anything else. Many people love the smell. Incense was already being made from it 2,000 years ago, and later perfumes. A lot of money is paid for it. But the tree makes the fragrant resin only when a certain type of fungus grows in its wood after its bark has been damaged. So basically the tree and the fungus together create the heavenly scent and bring in the money.

• "Stradivarius" is a word that will make any violinist drool. Italian violin-maker Antonio Stradivari's violins sound as fantastic as ever, even at 300 years old. Dutch violinist and composer André Rieu paid a couple million dollars for his. For centuries, everyone from the music world wondered what makes them sound so special. In 2008, the secret was revealed by a Swiss professor. He discovered something about the wood of the Stradivarius. The front of the sound box is made of spruce, the back of maple. That's not so special, but something had happened to the two woods. They'd had fungi in them: *Physisporinus vitreus* in the spruce, and dead moll's fingers (*Xylaria longipes*) in the maple. They had gnawed at it in such a way that the wood amplifies the sound of the strings much better than regular wood.

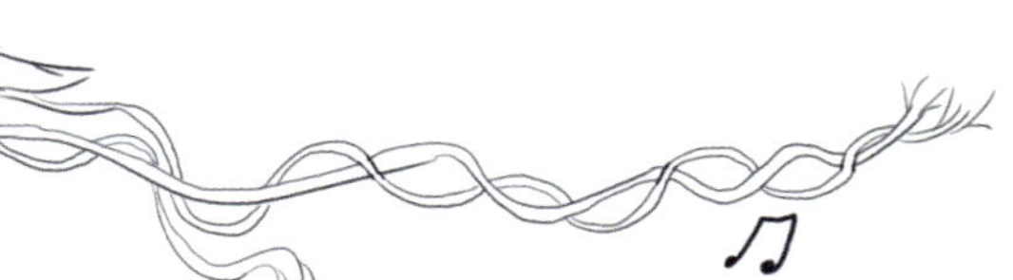

Name: **king bolete** | Scientific name: ***Boletus edulis***

There are no gills under its brown bowler hat, but holes. Or, more accurately, tubes. Beloved food of squirrels, Italians (who know these mushrooms as *porcini*), French (*cèpes*), and other gourmets.

# On your plate

Prehistoric people were already eating mushrooms. Not pan-fried with garlic, but raw or singed on hot coals. The Ancient Greeks loved mushrooms too. "God's bread," they called them. And the favorite dish of the Roman emperor Julius Caesar was *Amanita caesarea*, commonly known as Caesar's mushroom. It had a different name before Caesar singled it out, but it's kept this chic one.

Caesar's mushroom

king bolete

## Mushroom-pickers

Even today, a lot of wild mushrooms are still eaten. They are popular in North America, Asia, Africa, and Europe. People learn from each other which mushrooms are edible and which are not. In France, if in doubt, you can visit the pharmacy to have your basket of picked mushrooms checked. The pharmacists there are all mushroom experts; it's part of their training.

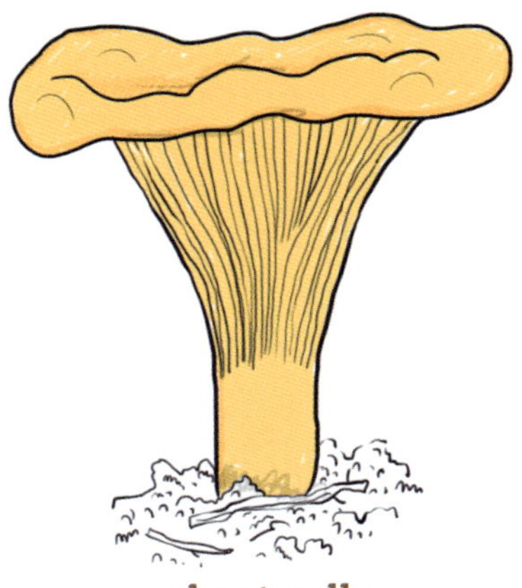
chanterelle

truffles

### Truffle-hunters

Truffles are very tasty but also very expensive. These fungi are hard to find because they grow underground. Truffle hunters use specially trained dogs or specially trained pigs to sniff them out. In Italy, truffle hunting is even a profession. You can get rich from it, because even the cheapest truffles can sell for more than $180 per pound ($400 per kilogram). About two pounds (a kilogram) of the most expensive truffle variety costs tens of thousands of dollars.

# Fungus farms

oyster mushrooms

The fungi that produce truffles, chanterelles, and king boletes live underground with tree roots in a forest. As a result, these mushrooms can't be cultivated. You can grow mushrooms that live on dead wood, however. Or mushrooms that grow on straw or horse poop. Button mushrooms love horse manure. In France, these mushrooms have been cultivated for 400 years. In Paris, mainly. It was the ideal place, because at the time, there were thousands of horses walking around, and they pooped a lot. What's more, there are a lot of caves and tunnels under the city. These were created when stones were dug out to build Parisian churches and palaces. The caves became ideal mushroom farms. The button mushroom is still the most cultivated mushroom in the world. American mushroom farms employ 21,000 people on around 300 farms; Canadian mushroom farms employ over 5,500 people.

Oyster mushrooms are often grown on straw, and shiitake on wood (sawdust). Two thousand years ago, people in China were already growing shiitake. Over 700 years ago, in 1313, shiitake-grower Wang Zeng wrote a detailed account of how he did this.

shiitake

button mushrooms

# Tasty fungal threads

Besides mushrooms, fungal threads are also eaten—but only when they are growing through something else. Cooked soybeans, for instance. Tempeh is the name for a block made of moldy soybeans. You can fry tempeh slices in soybean oil and then dip them in soy sauce (more on that later). Tasty, healthy, and totally vegan.

The best-known edible mold is in cheese. And not in an old chunk of Edam or Gouda that's gone off but in deliberately moldy cheeses from Denmark, England, or France. The cheese-maker plants the right kind of *Penicillium* on their unripe cheese and the mold turns it into an edible moldy cheese. The ones from France are particularly famous: soft cheese with a white layer of mold on the outside, like Brie and Camembert. And the stronger-tasting blue cheeses, like Roquefort. Their color comes from the blue mold spores. The molds don't add much bulk, but they do add a lot of flavor. That's their job.

***Penicillium roqueforti***

**Say cheese!**

**The fungal species *Penicillium roqueforti* is named after the cheese of the same name. Its sibling *Penicillium camemberti* is too.**

# Mold sauce

*Aspergillus sojae* is another flavoring. If you look at its second name, you might guess what this fungus likes to grow in. That's right: soybeans. If you leave it alone with some cooked soy for a few days and then put those moldy beans in salt water for a few months, you get soy sauce. The mold and salt release all kinds of tasty substances from the beans. This particular taste is described as *umami*, which in Japanese means "deliciousness."

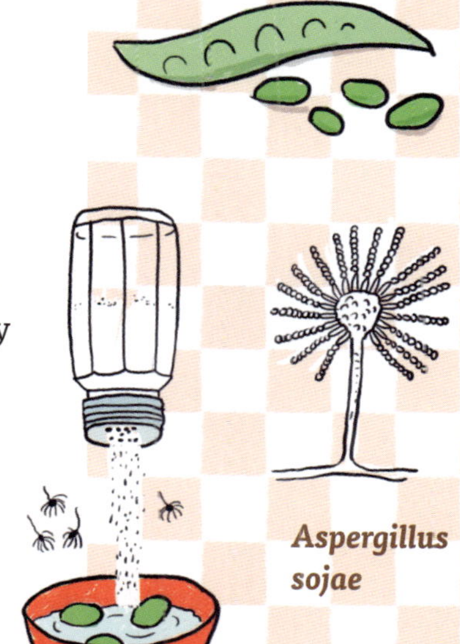

**Aspergillus sojae**

# Baking and brewing

You probably knew about yeast before reading this book. If you've ever baked bread, or doughnuts, yeast might have been in the recipe. You might have used dried yeast from a packet or, if you're a serious baker, a lump of fresh yeast. When you used that yeast, you stirred live fungi into the dough or batter. And once they are in there, in a warm place with a damp cloth over their heads, the yeast cells celebrate. They eat the sugar and flour; they grow fast and burp a lot. That's why bubbles appear. The mixture gets nice and fluffy. If you're making doughnuts you throw the batter into hot oil. The yeast cells don't survive that, but they did have fun in the last few hours of their lives.

Apart from baking bread and doughnuts, yeast also helps in brewing beer. That's how the bubbles get in beer, from the burping yeast cells. Instead of feeding the yeast flour, brewers give it watery barley goop. They put the yeast and the goop in a sealed brew kettle where there's not much oxygen. That stops the yeast from growing, but it doesn't stop them from eating the sugar from the barley. And they pee too. Special yeast pee, which we call alcohol.

Actually, all alcohol is made with the help of yeast. For wine, the yeast is fed grape juice, and for the alcohol in biofuel, it is fed sugarcane.

BURP

# Medicines and factories

Fungi are often used in medicines. Poisonous ones too, because poison, in small quantities, often actually works as medicine.

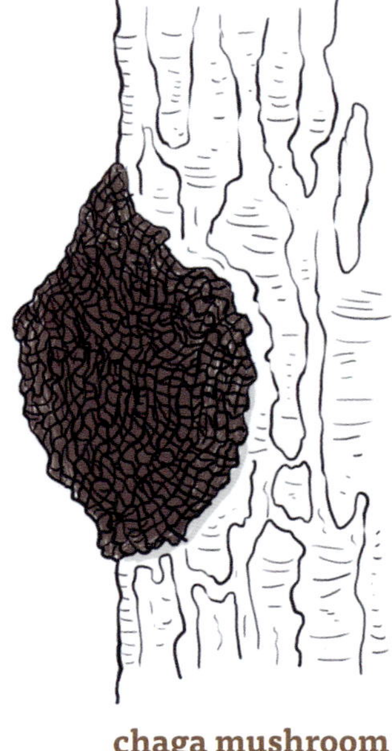

chaga mushroom

- Chaga mushrooms, orange peel fungus, wood ear, hoof fungus, hen-of-the-woods, turkey tail, and reishi are believed by some to fight cancer.
- Substances from *Aspergillus* fungus can help prevent heart attacks.
- Common inkcap and club-foot mushrooms can be eaten without any problems, but as soon as you take a sip of wine or other alcoholic beverage, you'll feel sick. Used in medicines, these mushrooms can help people with alcohol addiction.
- The best-known medicine made by a fungus is penicillin. This is an antibiotic: great for getting rid of bacteria in your body that are making you ill. It comes from the *Penicillium* fungus.

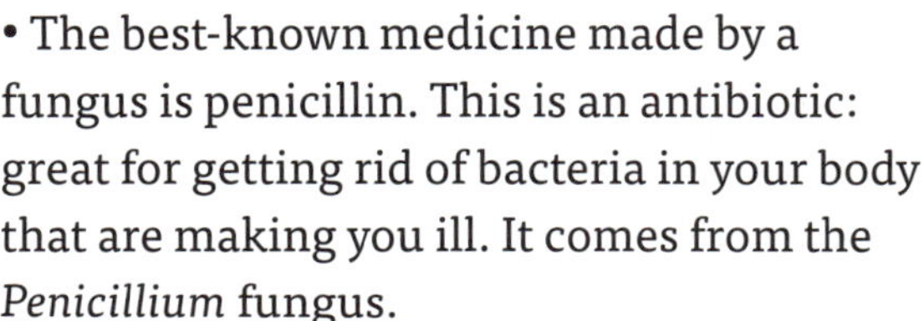

- There are even medicines made from fungi that work against fungal diseases.

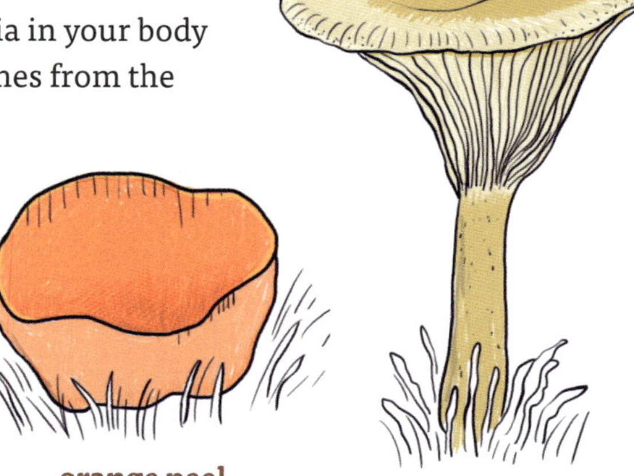

orange peel fungus

club-foot mushroom

common inkcap

hen-of-the-woods

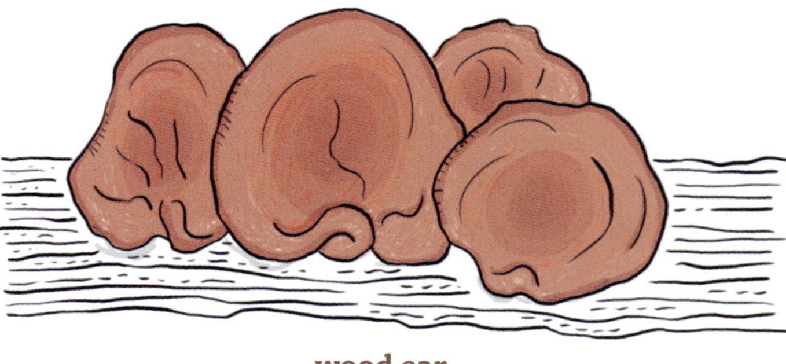

wood ear

## A careless discovery

Scottish bacterial biologist Alexander Fleming discovered in 1928 that *Penicillium* produces a powerful bacterial toxin. For his research, he was growing bacteria in dishes containing a kind of pudding that they could eat. One day, after returning to his tiny and crowded lab from a family holiday, he noticed something odd in the pile of petri dishes he'd left in the sink. One of them had tufts of *Penicillium* growing on it. The bacteria around each tuft had died. Fleming saw a bright future for the fungus. From World War II onward, penicillin became one of the world's most important medicines. It has saved millions of lives—all thanks to the careless but observant Sir Fleming, but mostly thanks to the penicillin itself.

***Penicillium* comes from the Latin word for "brush": *penicillus*. The fungus looks a bit like one, doesn't it?**

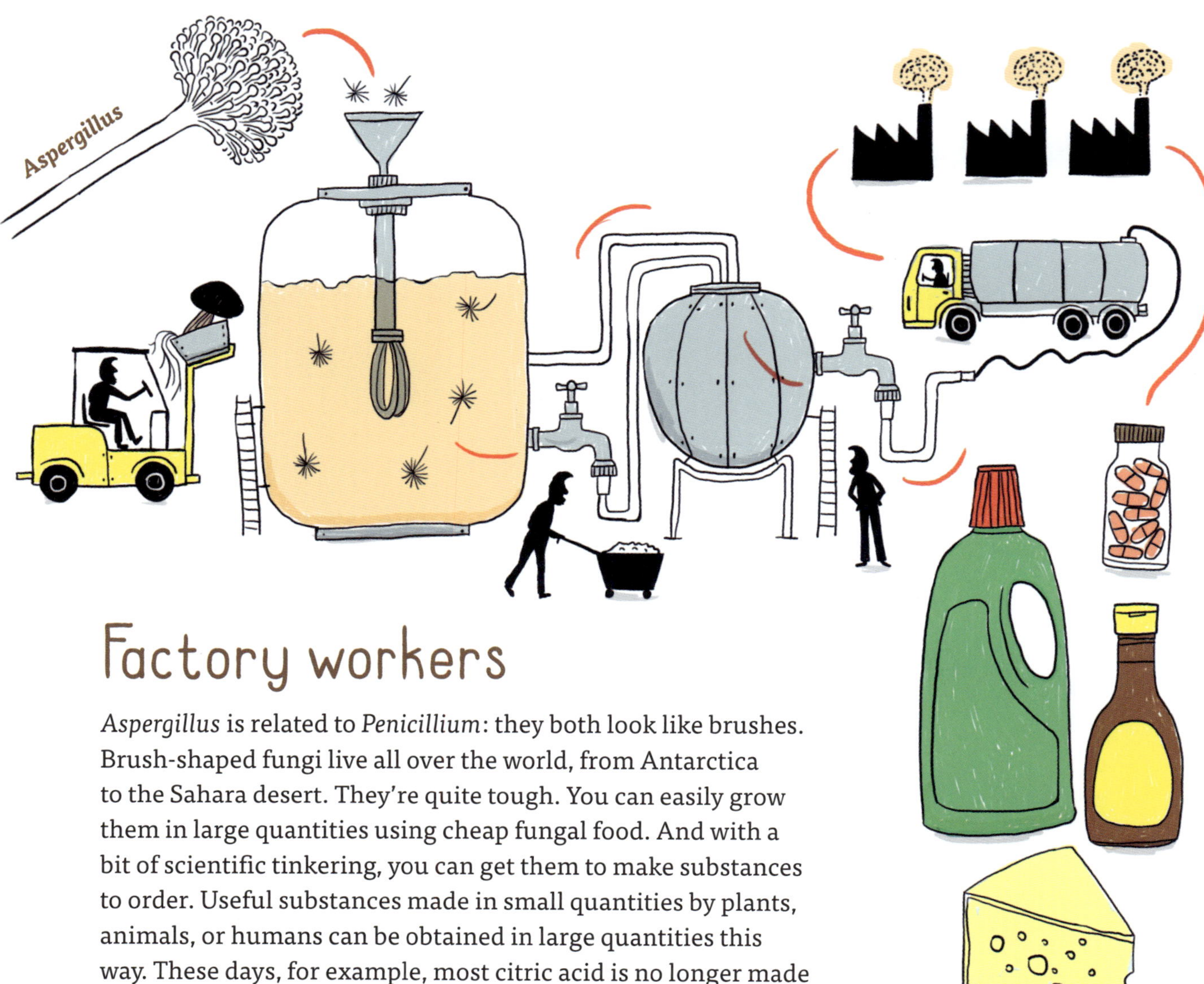


# Factory workers

*Aspergillus* is related to *Penicillium*: they both look like brushes. Brush-shaped fungi live all over the world, from Antarctica to the Sahara desert. They're quite tough. You can easily grow them in large quantities using cheap fungal food. And with a bit of scientific tinkering, you can get them to make substances to order. Useful substances made in small quantities by plants, animals, or humans can be obtained in large quantities this way. These days, for example, most citric acid is no longer made by lemon trees but by fungi, growing in big shiny cauldrons.

In factories, fungi are mainly put to work to make enzymes. An **enzyme** (en-zym) is a substance a living creature makes to quickly assemble other substances, or to quickly break down substances. There are lots of different kinds of enzymes, and they used to be expensive and hard to come by. Thanks to industrious fungi, however, they are now cheap and available in large quantities. Enzymes help make cheese, syrup, detergent, medicine, and much more. Thank you, *Aspergillus*!

***Aspergillus* spore carriers look suspiciously like toilet brushes. *Aspergillus* comes from the Latin word *aspergillum*, which means "holy water brush"—a reference to the tool Catholic priests use to sprinkle holy water during services.**

# High-tech fungi

In the future, fungi are likely to be used to make even more stuff. Clothes, for instance. We've always made them from threads, so why not from fungal threads? A Dutch fashion designer has made a dress from dried fungal mats. And there's already leather that isn't made from cow or sheep skin but from mushroom caps. It's totally vegan, and nice and stretchy and airy, making you less prone to fungal infections between your toes.

Dead fungal threads break down naturally in nature, but plastic does not. Some factories are already growing fungi to make lightweight packaging: plastic-free Styrofoam, which is very good for transporting computers. And how about a coffin made from living molds? This already exists too—excellent for the soil and less heavy to carry.

Some fungi can break down wood, something no other living creature can do. And some fungi are already prepared for the next challenge: eating plastic. The oyster mushroom, for example, seems to have what it takes—and we can enjoy eating it after its work is done.

# Weapons and drugs

Like bullets, bombs, and grenades, fungi can cause death and destruction. Not surprisingly, they have also been used in wars, although countries will usually not admit to it. The *Fusarium* fungus makes a deadly poison. Americans in Vietnam and Russians in Afghanistan sprayed this dangerous yellow stuff over enemy territory from a plane. They weren't worried about their own safety because the "yellow rain" wears off after 24 hours.

liberty caps

Dried liberty caps are sold as "magic truffles."

## Magic mushrooms

The substances in some mushrooms do strange things to your brain. These mushrooms are known as "magic mushrooms." They grow all over the world, including in North America, where you can find liberty caps. Some are grown and then deliberately stressed with not enough water or too much heat so much they make "survival capsules" (see page 41). The capsules' hard outer shell makes them easy to store and ship, and liberty caps are sold in some specialty stores.

It is not safe to take magic mushrooms. They can make you do strange things, which can be dangerous for you and for those around you. Because of this, it is illegal to take, possess, or sell magic mushrooms in many places, including most of North America and many countries in Europe.

### Ancient magic mushrooms

There are 10,000-year-old drawings of mushrooms on cave walls in North Africa. According to experts, these are magic mushrooms. That would make sense. In Central America, dozens of ancient stone sculptures made by Mayans have been found. They look like men with sort of pointy hats. But are they gnomes? No, they're mushrooms with faces.

# Researchers and protectors

Many scientists have been interested in fungi. One of the first researchers was Johanna Westerdijk. In 1917 this fungal biologist became the first female professor in the Netherlands. She founded a laboratory at Utrecht University, and important fungal research is still done there today.

The famous British children's author and illustrator Beatrix Potter was fascinated by natural history. She made many excellent drawings of fungi and was one of the first known people in the world to cultivate them from spores.

**The study of fungi is called mycology (my-coll-oh-gee). A fungal scientist is a mycologist.**

If you're not a baker or a brewer, baker's yeast doesn't seem that interesting. Under a microscope, a yeast cell is nothing more than a glob—or two circles joined together, if the cell is dividing. But many scientists are interested. Yeast cells behave in quite a similar way to human cells, and they reproduce at lightning speed, so you can do all kinds of experiments with them. For example, you can test how drugs work. Baker's yeast has helped biologists, doctors, chemists, and pharmacists a lot. It is one of the most studied species in the world, and its researchers have won six Nobel Prizes.

# Excited biologists

The biggest kick for a mushroom biologist is, of course, finding a new species. In some areas, it's not even that difficult. In most rainforests, mushrooms haven't yet been well researched. But even in Western countries, there is still a lot to discover. North America has around 11,000 species of mushroom, but hundreds of new ones are described each year.

Biologists keep track on maps of where they have found which mushroom. Regularly, they find a species new to a country. Most of these were probably already there, but they've only just been found because more people are paying attention. But some species are no longer found. This is because of changes in nature due to climate change, pollution, and development. In recent years, hundreds of species of mushrooms have disappeared. Many more mushrooms that used to be common have now become rare.

# A warning system

Fungi help us by telling us something about the environment. Lichens are worth watching for signs of air pollution, especially lichens that grow on trees. When these disappear, you know something's wrong. As far back as half a century ago, they led scientists to issue warnings that there was too much sulfur in the air. It was coming from dirty oil and coal. Measures were adopted to address this issue. Now nitrogen is a big problem. Some people think it's not that bad, but fungi don't lie.

CAN'T BREATHE!

Fungi and people are connected in so many ways. Mushrooms, in particular, keep many people busy. Thanks to all that you've learned while reading this book, you could be one of those people. Keep reading to find out how you can get more involved with the amazing world of fungi!

# 7 DO IT YOURSELF

Congratulations! You're well on your way to becoming a mushroom pro and a fungus expert. But the fun doesn't have to stop when you're finished reading this book. You can also get out there and explore. Like in the first chapter, mushrooms are the center of attention in this final chapter too. There's so much more to learn about what's behind—and underneath—each one!

# Search and find

Start by looking at mushrooms. Or rather, looking for them. How do you go about that? And, most important, when and where? It all depends on what you want. The good news is you can find mushrooms in most places and in all seasons. If you like nature, you don't even need to go looking for them. You'll just come across them when you are out hiking or bird-watching or looking at plants.

## Go hiking with an expert

Want to get really serious? Then take advantage of people who already know their stuff. Sign up with a local mycological society for a mushroom tour or foraging trip (you can search on the internet for groups in your area). That way, you'll get tips on how to identify them and where the best places are to look. A guide often has years of experience, so don't be afraid to pick their brains. They also know *where* you're allowed to pick mushrooms; it's not legal everywhere. Listen carefully, take notes, and take pictures. And then make up your own system so that you know which name belongs to which picture when you look back at them.

Autumn and the forest are the best time and place for mushrooms. But there are good and bad mushroom years. Again, the best thing is to keep an eye on the experts. Find a few experts or a club in your area and follow them on Facebook or Instagram, for example. If there are lots of mushrooms somewhere, they might share that info.

# Look under the cap

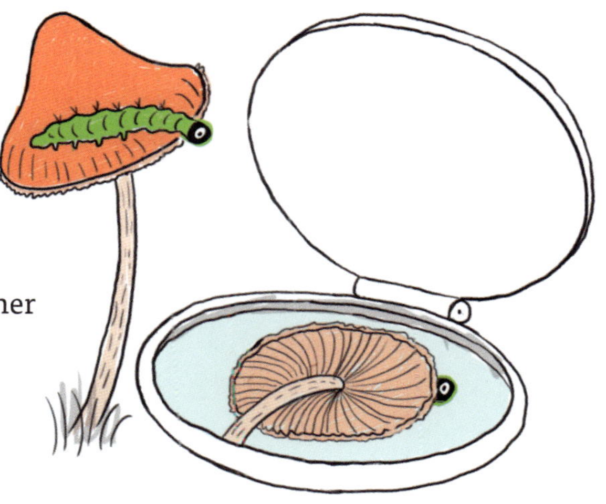

If you go out looking for mushrooms, always take a mirror with you. Unless you are a gnome, it's hard to look under their caps. Putting your cheek on the wet ground is no fun, and it's better not to pick the mushrooms. But why would you want to look underneath? Well, what's under the cap tells you a lot about which mushroom you've found: whether it's an agaric or another type (see page 38). So a mirror is really handy, and the smallest mirror you can get is big enough.

A magnifying glass is also handy, but not totally necessary. That's really for advanced mushroomers. Biologists, for example, have magnifying glasses that enlarge things 10 to 20 times. You really need to practice looking through one of those. If you are going to make a wish list, though, ask for a magnifying glass with an LED light; it will let you see more. But if you don't have a magnifying glass, don't let that stop you from exploring: most young people can see clearly up close even without help.

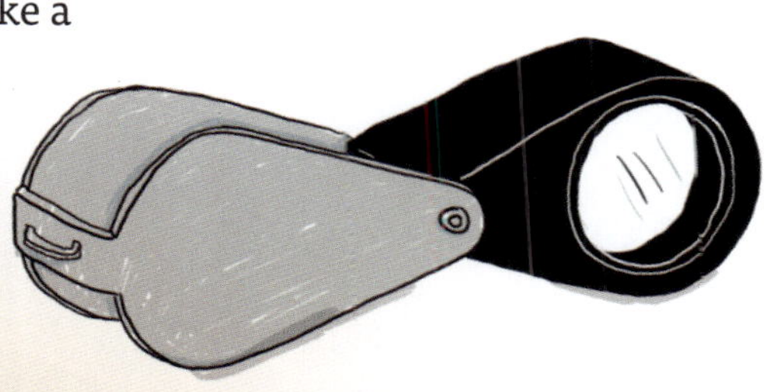

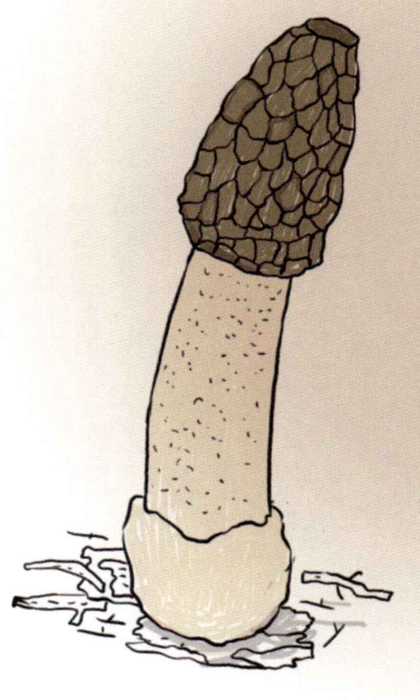

# Smell and taste

Getting up close to mushrooms is important: besides what you can see with your eyes, a good nose also comes in handy when you want to know which species you're looking at. It's hard to describe a smell, but if you can make a few notes about it, it will be useful in the future.

And tasting? Well, real mushroom experts do that. A tiny chunk at the front of the mouth. Is it sour, bitter, peppery, or nutty? Afterward, they spit out the chunk. But leave that to the experts for now: Don't go sinking your teeth into any unknown mushrooms!

# Books, websites, and apps

You've already got a copy of *Mushrooms and Company*, but if you're serious about mushroom hunting, you'll need another book: a mushroom guide. Books like that can be expensive, and not all of them are very useful. Before buying a mushroom guide or asking for one as a gift, it's best to try it out first. Try borrowing one from the library. The best guides are in the adult section, under "nature," probably, and, if you're lucky, on the "mushrooms" shelf.

There are also apps with information and photos, and sometimes with photo recognition. This can be useful, but they aren't always accurate. Some apps are free and good; others are expensive and bad. And it's important to find one that's specific to your area. An American or Australian app is of little use in Europe, and vice versa.

Name: **fly agaric** | Scientific name: ***Amanita muscaria***
Red with white spots but doesn't always keep its colors; the rain can wash them out a bit. When the cap grows, the spots get farther apart. Some even wash off.

# Questions, questions, questions!

If you've found a mushroom and want to know what species it is, these questions will help. The more answers you can give, the more likely you are to find the name of your discovery in a mushroom guide or on a website—and, most of all, the more certain you'll be about which species it is.

## Which mushroom is it?

### What shape is it?

- standard (with cap and stalk)
- round
- semicircle (growing on wood)
- other

### Where is it growing?

- forest
- do I recognize the nearby trees?
- in the grass
- other

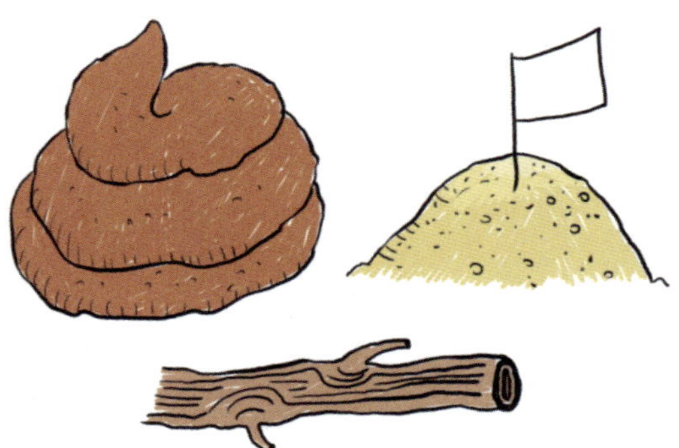

### What is it growing on?

- out of the ground
- on wood
- on poop
- other

### What color is the cap?

- on the top?
- on the underside?
- does the color change when I pinch it?
- does it have dots or stripes?
- does juice come out when I break off a piece? If so, what color?

### What shape is the cap?

- flat
- round
- pointy
- long and thin
- other

### What is the top of the cap like?

- dry or slippery?
- smooth or scaly?
- other

### What's under the cap?

- gills
- tubes
- tiny holes
- spines
- is there any powder underneath? If so, what color?

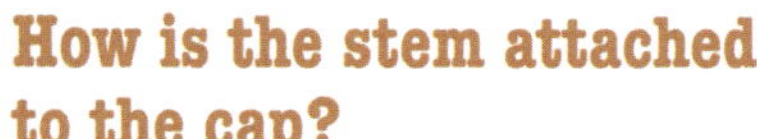

### How is the stem attached to the cap?

- in the middle
- to one side
- other

### What does it smell like?

- nothing
- nasty, like . . .
- nice, like . . .

### What does the stem look like?

- is it thick or thin?
- is it equally thick (or thin) everywhere?
- is it bulbous at the bottom?
- does it have a ring around it?
- other

# Fake it till you make it: A bluffer's guide to mushrooms

Nobody knows all of the thousands of species of mushrooms in the world. You won't be able to learn them all either. But you can memorize a few easily recognizable common species. Or even the main species groups. If you do that, you'll be able to name a lot of mushrooms. Not their full name, but the type. You could say: "That's a bolete." Or, if you're very honest: "I think it's a bolete, but I'm not sure which one." Another advantage: once you know the species type, it's easier to find it in a mushroom guide. Usually the members of a group are listed together.

## Bluff your way through the fungi

This book isn't a mushroom textbook, and it's certainly not a mushroom guide. You won't become an expert overnight, but you can make a start with these bluffing tips. And you might even impress some people.

Say "a fly agaric" when you see the kind from fairytales.

Say "an *Amanita*" (am-uh-nee-ta) when the mushroom looks like a fly agaric—with spots and a ring—but isn't red with white dots.

Say "an inkcap" if it has black gunk coming out from under the cap. The one you'll see most often is the shaggy ink-cap, with its tall, ragged cap.

Say "a bolete" if it is a mushroom with a thick stem and tubes under the cap.

Say "a *Mycena*" (my-see-na) to any tiny brown mushrooms with a long, thin stalk.

Say "a stem decay fungus" or "a bracket fungus" to half-caps growing like balconies on living or dead tree trunks. And "a turkey tail" if it has light and dark rings.

Say "a milk cap" if white or colored sap comes out when you break a piece of the cap.

Say "a *Russula*" to a colorful mushroom whose white stem crumbles when you squeeze it.

Say "a puffball" to balls on the ground. If they are old and puff out dust when you pinch them, you'll know for sure. If it's yellow and bounces, it's a tennis ball!

Say "a stinkhorn" to one of these tall fellas giving off a nasty whiff.

Say "a bird's nest fungus" to a cup-like formation with tiny white "eggs" inside.

A couple of giants you should know:

- a dinosaur's egg in a meadow: "a giant puffball"

- a white umbrella in the grass: "a parasol mushroom"

# Collect and examine

Can you pick mushrooms to study them? That seems like a tricky question, but it really isn't. All you have to do is think about other people who might be interested in mushrooms too.

A mushroom that you've picked and taken away can't be seen by anybody else. If there are only a few beautiful mushrooms growing in a place that lots of people go past, consider examining them using your little mirror and taking a photo instead of picking them.

Although other people might not like it if you pick too many mushrooms just to get a better look, the fungus itself doesn't mind. The fungal network suffers more from people walking on it than from having its mushrooms picked. So, if you're really going to do something with it, feel free to pick the occasional mushroom.

You can keep tough mushrooms—like bracket fungi—for your own natural history collection. But put them in the freezer for two days first, and then again after a few days. It will prevent maggots from eating your museum piece from the inside out.

# A handy print

Some mushroom guides ask for the color of the spores. In nature, however, it can be very difficult to tell. With bracket mushrooms, you might sometimes see a bit of colored powder on them: the spores of their upstairs neighbor. But usually, you'll have to make a spore print to find out. You can find instructions for doing this just below, but you do have to take the cap home for this project, so only do it if you are allowed and if you want to pick the mushroom.

## How to make a spore print

### You'll need

- white paper (to look at dark-colored spores)
- dark-colored paper (to look at light-colored spores)
- the cap of a mushroom
- a glass

### Instructions

1. Put the cap half on the white paper and half on the dark paper.
2. Put the glass over the cap to prevent drafts (spores blow away easily).
3. Leave it overnight.
4. In the morning, carefully lift the glass and the cap.

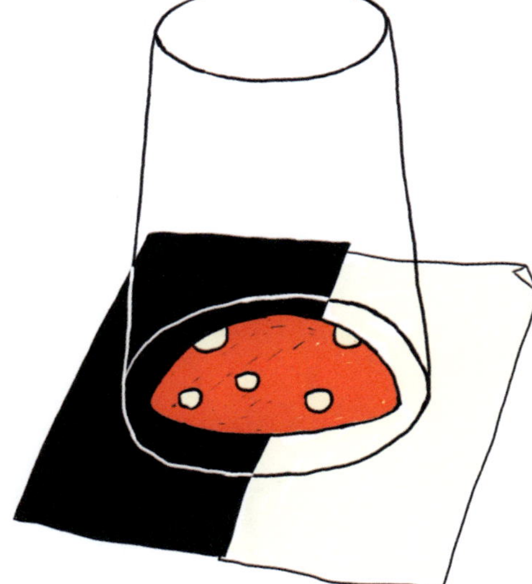

If you can see the pattern of the bottom of the cap on your paper, your spore print has worked and you'll be able to see what color the spores are! Take a picture of it. If you want to keep the print, place transparent tape over it.

# A special viewing box

Spores in the air are much too small to see. But with a flashlight and a shoebox, you can still make them visible for a while.

## How to make and use a spore viewing box

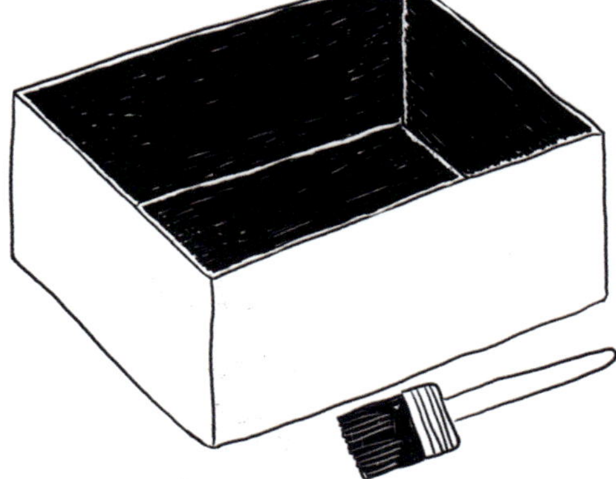

### You'll need

- a shoebox
- scissors or a perforating tool (or a knife, and then help from an adult)
- black paint, preferably matte
- a flashlight (a smartphone light will also do)
- a mushroom cap

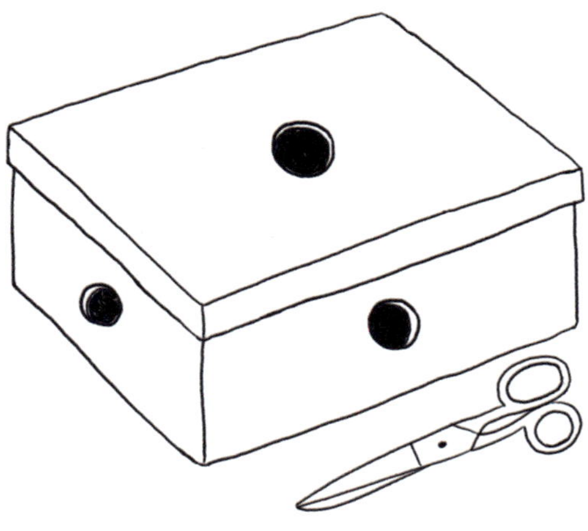

### Instructions for making the box

1 Paint the inside of the shoebox black.
2 Let it dry.
3 Carefully poke three holes in the box (ask an adult for help): one on the top, one on a long side, and one on a short side.

### How to use it (preferably in a dark room)

1 Place the cap over the top hole.
2 Shine the light through the hole on the long side of the box.
3 Look through the hole on the short side of the box.
4 Tap the cap.
5 Watch the spores swirl!

# Grow your own

Do you want to grow your own edible mushrooms? Most species are too difficult to grow, even for a pro. But a few species do well, and you can buy special cultivation kits on the internet or from a garden center. They tell you exactly what to do. Most sets are quite simple. Waiting for the first mushrooms to appear is probably the hardest part. For a species that grows on wood, you buy a piece of trunk, sometimes called "edible wood." Oak with shiitake, for example. Or a pot of wood chips with oyster mushroom threads already living in it. Growing them is fun, and they're tasty too. If you do it right, you'll be able to pick the mushrooms for a few years.

# Quick threads

Growing fungal threads is easy. It sometimes happens by accident: in a forgotten lunch box or the fruit bowl. Before you read this book, you used to throw away a moldy sandwich or a blue orange in disgust. Now, though, you'll have a good look at it first (maybe with your new magnifying glass!). Just be careful: don't breathe in too deeply—it's best to wear a mask—because inhaling a cloud of spores is not healthy, even for young lungs. After you've had a good look, you can put the sandwich or the orange or whatever was growing the fungi in the compost bin, with the rest of the organic waste. If it happens to be a hot summer day, you'll probably find more fungi in there too. Sometimes, within a day, a huge tangle of white threads with black bobbles can grow inside. A miracle!

# Smart feasting

You've read quite a bit about edible mushrooms in this book, and about poisonous ones too. It's important not to mix them up if you want to eat mushrooms!

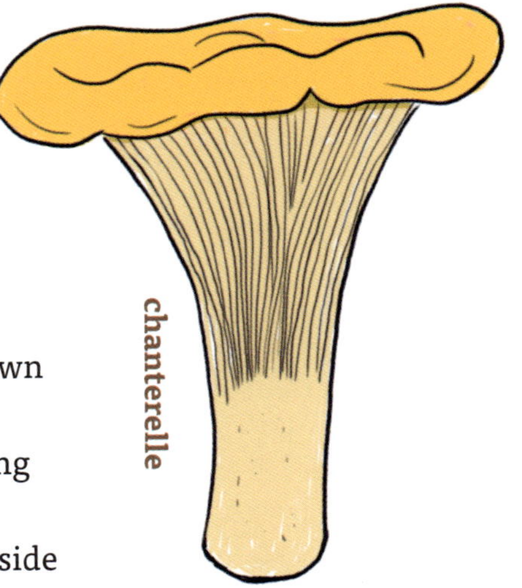


## Finding and picking

Do you want to head out to the countryside and pick your own mushrooms? Always do this with a real mushroom expert. Someone you trust 100 percent. Someone who can tell a king bolete from a Satan's bolete. And even king boletes are not always okay. If the mushroom is growing in the ditch alongside a highway, it will be tasty but not very healthy.

Mistakes are often made with chanterelles. In fact, the false chanterelle looks very similar to the real thing. Both of these can be found in North America. Fortunately, the false chanterelle isn't poisonous, but it's not very tasty either.

## Buying mushrooms

If you want to eat mushrooms but aren't sure about picking your own, the safest thing to do is to buy them. Every supermarket has white and brown mushrooms. Many sell other varieties too, like oyster mushrooms and shiitake. Or a box of a few varieties together. For the more unusual ones, you'll probably need to go to a market, preferably a farmers market, where there is sometimes a stall selling cultivated or wild-picked mushrooms. Whole trays of chanterelles. They aren't cheap—you can count on paying five times as much as you would for mushrooms in the supermarket. But they are ten times as tasty. You can use them for a special dish, like a fragrant rice or a fancy pasta.

Dried mushrooms can be bought at big supermarkets—just search or ask—and at some delis or stores selling Asian groceries. Buy them as soon as you see them: you can keep them for a long time. Dried king boletes are especially delicious.

**Clever marketing**

You can also find portobello mushrooms in the supermarket. These are button mushrooms that have grown some more and have an open cap. Not so long ago, no one wanted to buy them. But then, in the 1980s, a clever marketing strategy gave them this new and glamorous name. Now they are popular—and extra expensive!

# Tips from a chef

- Never wash fresh mushrooms with water. It will flush a lot of flavor down the drain. Instead, use a vegetable brush to clean them.

- Dried mushrooms should be put in water for a while. Half an hour is long enough. Take them out and pat them dry. But save the tasty brown water and add it to your dish later when cooking.

- You can cut fresh mushrooms into neat slices using an egg slicer.

# The ultimate test

You've almost finished the book. When you started it, you probably thought it was only about mushrooms. Now you know better: *Mushrooms and Company* is about so much more than that. It's about the networks of which each mushroom is just one small part. It's about an entire kingdom—the fungal kingdom—which is as rich as the animal kingdom and the plant kingdom. You've realized that fungi are not boring at all but are important contributors to the world around them. They are hard workers too—sometimes for the good, and sometimes stirring up trouble. There's even something human about them. Which means the reverse is also true: every human is a bit like a fungus. Of course, there are lots of different fungi, and lots of different people. To see which fungi you are most like, take the quiz below.

## Which fungus are you?

I like deciduous forests more than coniferous forests.
Yes
No
You are a pinecone cap.
I can handle the cold.
Yes
No
BRRRRRR
You are a witch's butter.
You are a veiled lady.
My room is full of plants.
Yes
No
You are a lichen.
I always clean up my dog's poop.
POOP
Yes
No
You are a common pinmold.
You are a fly agaric.
Yes
No
I'm famous, everyone knows me (though not everyone knows my name).
You are like countless other fungi. You might be troublesome at times, but probably the people who know you are glad you're there. Without you, the world wouldn't be complete. And who knows, maybe one day you'll become a famous fungus expert!

# Glossary

**agaric**
A *mushroom* with *gills* under the cap.

**antibiotics**
Substances that are fatally toxic to bacteria.

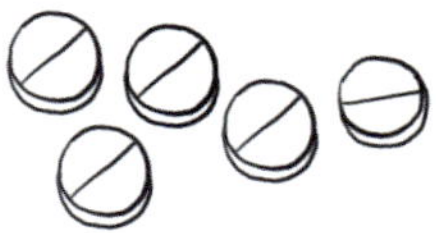

**athlete's foot**
Skin disease caused by foot fungus.

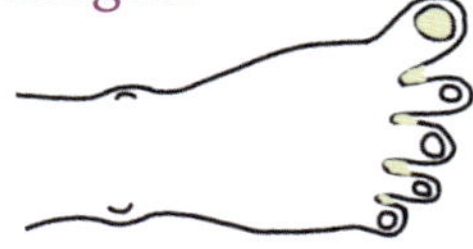

**blight**
Plant disease caused by a *fungus*.

**brown rot**
A type of decay that leaves rotten wood that is brown and crumbly, caused by a wood fungus that digests only *cellulose*.

**cell**
The smallest unit of life.

**cell nucleus**
Spherical "brain" inside the *cell*. More than one called "cell nuclei."

**cellulose**
Hard-to-digest substance that plants are full of.

**cell wall**
Solid shell of a plant cell, mainly made of *cellulose*.

**chitin**
Substance that gives strength to *fungi*. The outer covering (exoskeleton) of insects, spiders, and shellfish also contains a lot of chitin.

**chlorophyll**
The green substance in plants and algae that allows them to use sunlight to make their own food (sugar) from water and carbon dioxide.

**club fungus**
*Mushroom* in which the *spores* grow on thin stalks. Usually four grow on one mother cell. A basidiomycete.

**enzyme**
A substance a living thing makes to quickly assemble or quickly break down certain other substances.

**fairy ring**
A circle of *mushrooms* on the ground.

**fungus**
A simple organism, or living thing, that is neither a plant nor an animal. When there is more than one fungus they are called "fungi." *Mushrooms*, *molds*, *mildews*, *truffles*, and *yeasts* are all fungi.

**gasteroid fungus**
A *puffball mushroom*.

**gills**
The flaps under the cap of an *agaric* where *spores* are made. Also called "lamellae."

**humus**
Soil with decayed bits of dead plants, dead leaves, and dead wood.

**hypha**
Fungal thread. More than one called "hyphae."

**lichen**
At least two different species, a *fungus* and an alga (along with bacteria), living together as one organism in a close *symbiotic* relationship.

**lignin**
A very difficult-to-digest substance that gives wood its strength.

**mildew**
*Fungus* that grows on a flat surface like a leaf.

**mold**
The furry growth of tiny *fungi* you find in warm, damp places, usually on food or other organic matter.

**mushroom**
A large (compared to the *hyphae*) and often unusually shaped *spore* carrier of a *fungus*.

**mycelium**
The *hyphal* network of one *fungus*. More than one called "mycelia."

**mycology**
The study of *fungi*.

**mycorrhiza**
The cooperative network of *fungi* fused with roots of trees or other plants. More than one called "mycorrhizae."

**peridiole**
A *spore* package resembling a little egg that some *fungi* make in a nest-like cup.

**primordium**
A kind of egg that contains a ready-made *mushroom*.

**puffball mushroom**
*Mushroom* that makes the *spores* inside its "belly" and bursts open when ripe. A *gasteroid fungus*.

**rust**
Plant disease caused by a *fungus*.

**sac fungus**
*Mushroom* in which the *spores* grow in elongated sacs. There are usually eight in one sac (like a pod with eight beans). An ascomycete.

**sclerotium**
A survival capsule of a *fungus*. More than one called "sclerotia."

**smut**
Plant disease caused by a *fungus*.

**sponge fungus**
A *mushroom* with holes under the cap. Basically a tube mushroom with tight tubes.

**spore**
A single fungal *cell* that acts like a plant seed but is much smaller. *Fungi* make spores, and so do mosses and ferns.

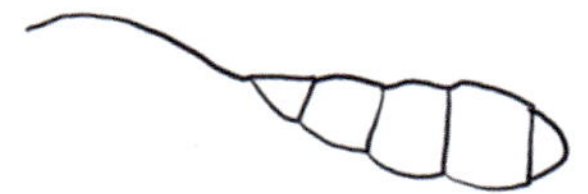

**symbiosis**
When two or more different species live together.

**tooth fungus**
A *mushroom* that makes *spores* on spikes hanging under its cap.

**truffle**
A *fungus* that grows underground. Specially trained animals sniff out their *spores* and spread them by pooping them out. Some truffles are very expensive!

**tube fungus**
A *mushroom* that makes *spores* within tubes under its cap. A polypore or bracket fungus.

**white rot**
A type of decay that leaves rotten wood that is soft and pale, caused by a wood fungus that digests mainly *lignin*.

**wood wide web**
All networks of *mycorrhizal mycelium* in a forest.

**yeast**
Single-celled type of *fungus*.

# Index

## R



## S



## T



## U



## V



## W



## Y



## Z